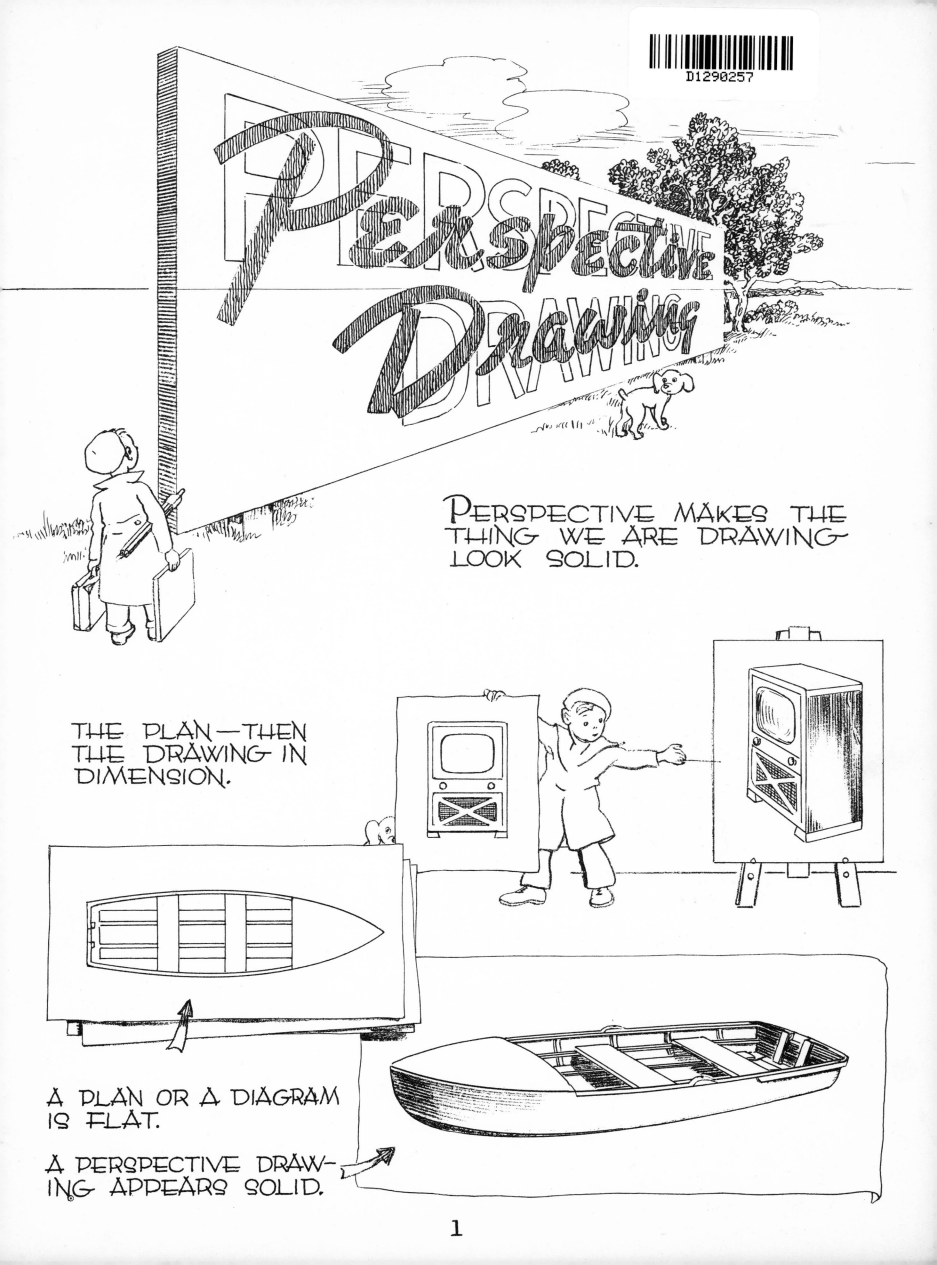

Perspective Drawing

PERSPECTIVE MAKES THE THING WE ARE DRAWING LOOK SOLID.

THE PLAN—THEN THE DRAWING IN DIMENSION.

A PLAN OR A DIAGRAM IS FLAT.

A PERSPECTIVE DRAWING APPEARS SOLID.

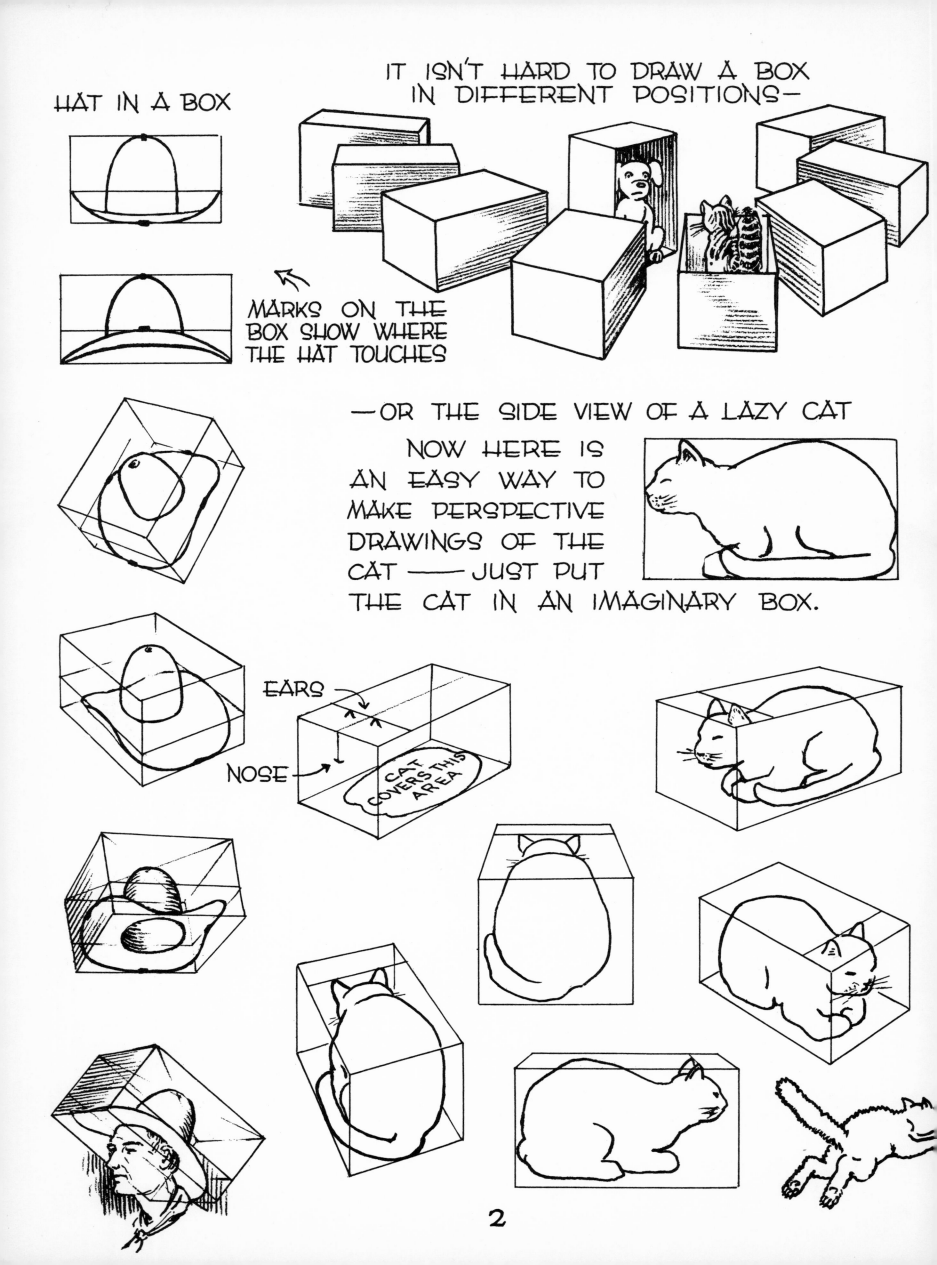

HAT IN A BOX

MARKS ON THE BOX SHOW WHERE THE HAT TOUCHES

IT ISN'T HARD TO DRAW A BOX IN DIFFERENT POSITIONS—

—OR THE SIDE VIEW OF A LAZY CAT

NOW HERE IS AN EASY WAY TO MAKE PERSPECTIVE DRAWINGS OF THE CAT —— JUST PUT THE CAT IN AN IMAGINARY BOX.

EARS

NOSE

CAT COVERS THIS AREA

YOU WILL FIND THAT MANY
THINGS CAN BE EASILY DRAWN
IN PERSPECTIVE BY PLACING THEM
IN BOXES.

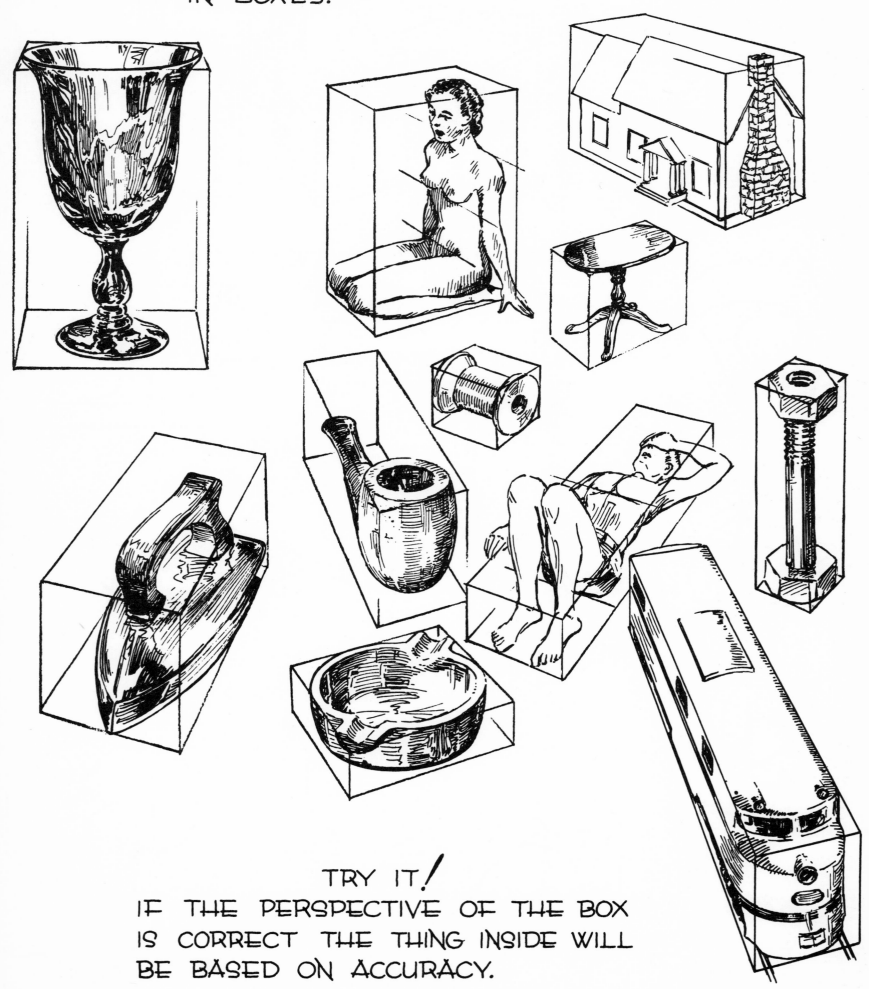

TRY IT!
IF THE PERSPECTIVE OF THE BOX
IS CORRECT THE THING INSIDE WILL
BE BASED ON ACCURACY.

BEFORE DRAWING A BOX LET US INVESTIGATE THE EYE LEVEL

HEIGHT OF ARTIST'S EYES FROM THE GROUND

THIS IS THE PICTURE THAT ARTIST WANTS TO PAINT

THIS IS WHERE THE ARTIST SEES THE HORIZON ON HIS CANVAS.

A CHILD'S EYE LEVEL

THE FINISHED PICTURE

THE ARTIST, IF HE WISHES, CAN TURN TO ANY DIRECTION — NORTH, SOUTH, EAST OR WEST. THE HORIZON WILL ALWAYS BE AT HIS EYE LEVEL.

NO MATTER HOW HIGH HE GETS.

— OR HOW LOW — THE HORIZON WILL ALWAYS BE AT HIS EYE LEVEL.

A GROWN UP'S EYE LEVEL

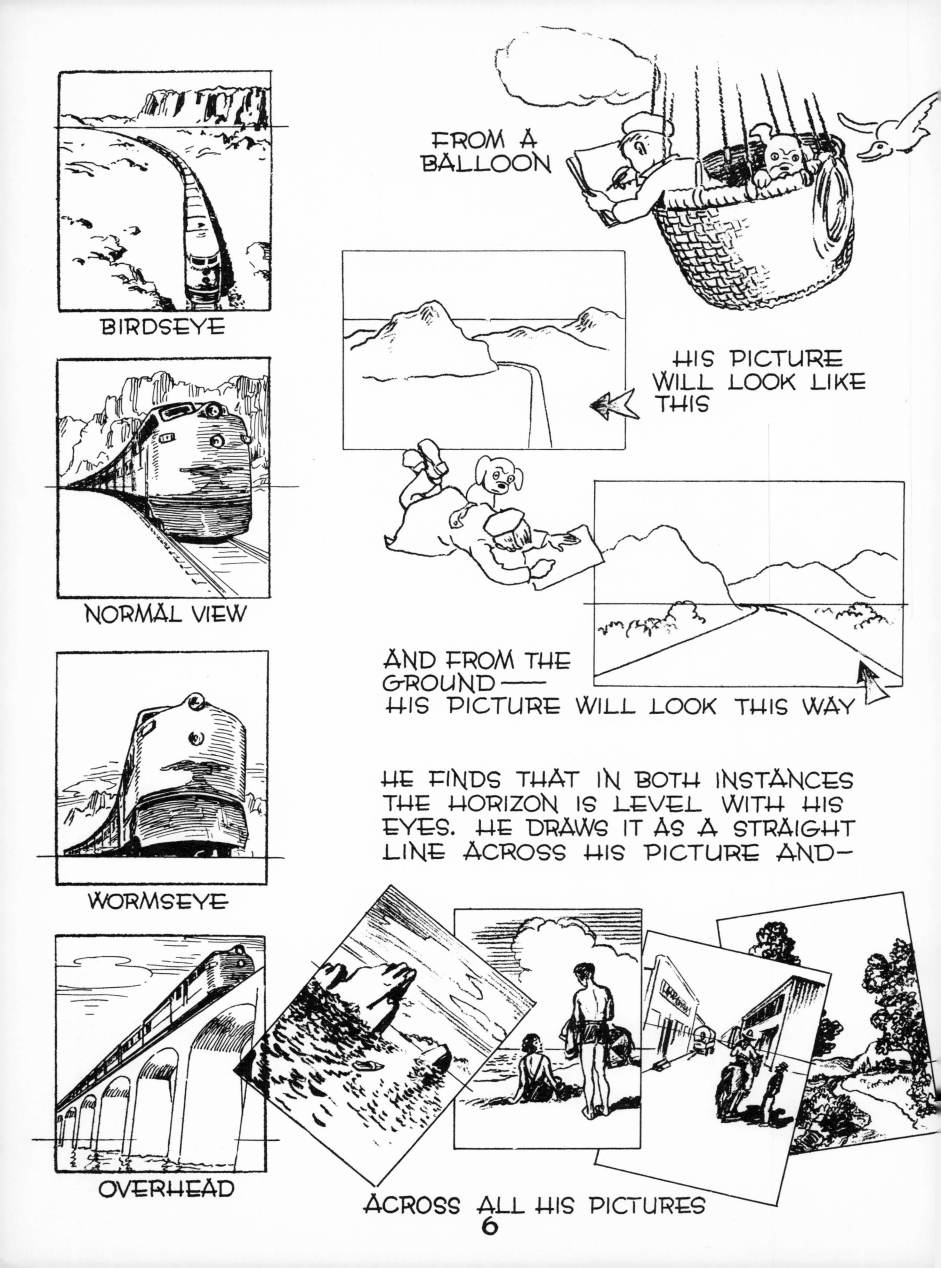

BIRDSEYE

NORMAL VIEW

WORMSEYE

OVERHEAD

FROM A BALLOON

HIS PICTURE WILL LOOK LIKE THIS

AND FROM THE GROUND—
HIS PICTURE WILL LOOK THIS WAY

HE FINDS THAT IN BOTH INSTANCES THE HORIZON IS LEVEL WITH HIS EYES. HE DRAWS IT AS A STRAIGHT LINE ACROSS HIS PICTURE AND—

ACROSS ALL HIS PICTURES

6

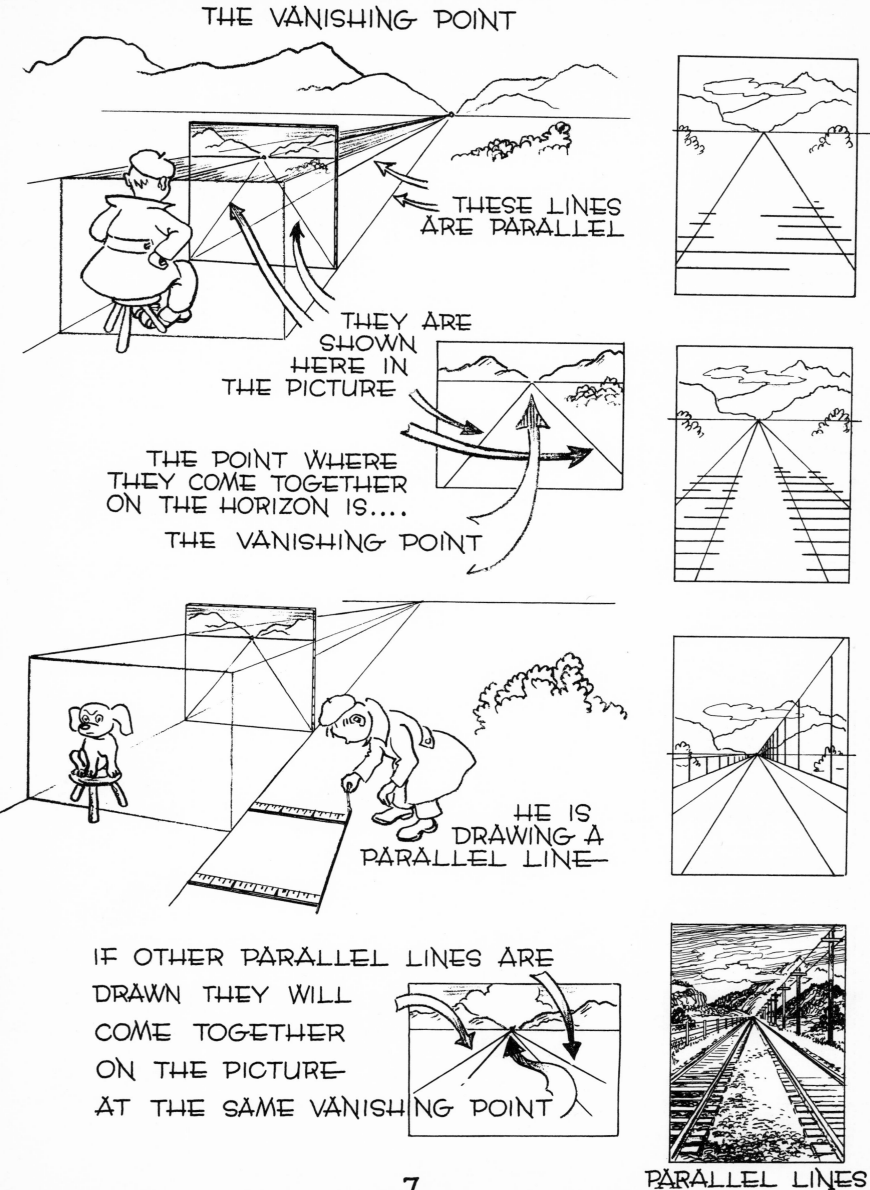

THE VANISHING POINT

THESE LINES ARE PARALLEL

THEY ARE SHOWN HERE IN THE PICTURE

THE POINT WHERE THEY COME TOGETHER ON THE HORIZON IS....

THE VANISHING POINT

HE IS DRAWING A PARALLEL LINE

IF OTHER PARALLEL LINES ARE DRAWN THEY WILL COME TOGETHER ON THE PICTURE AT THE SAME VANISHING POINT

PARALLEL LINES

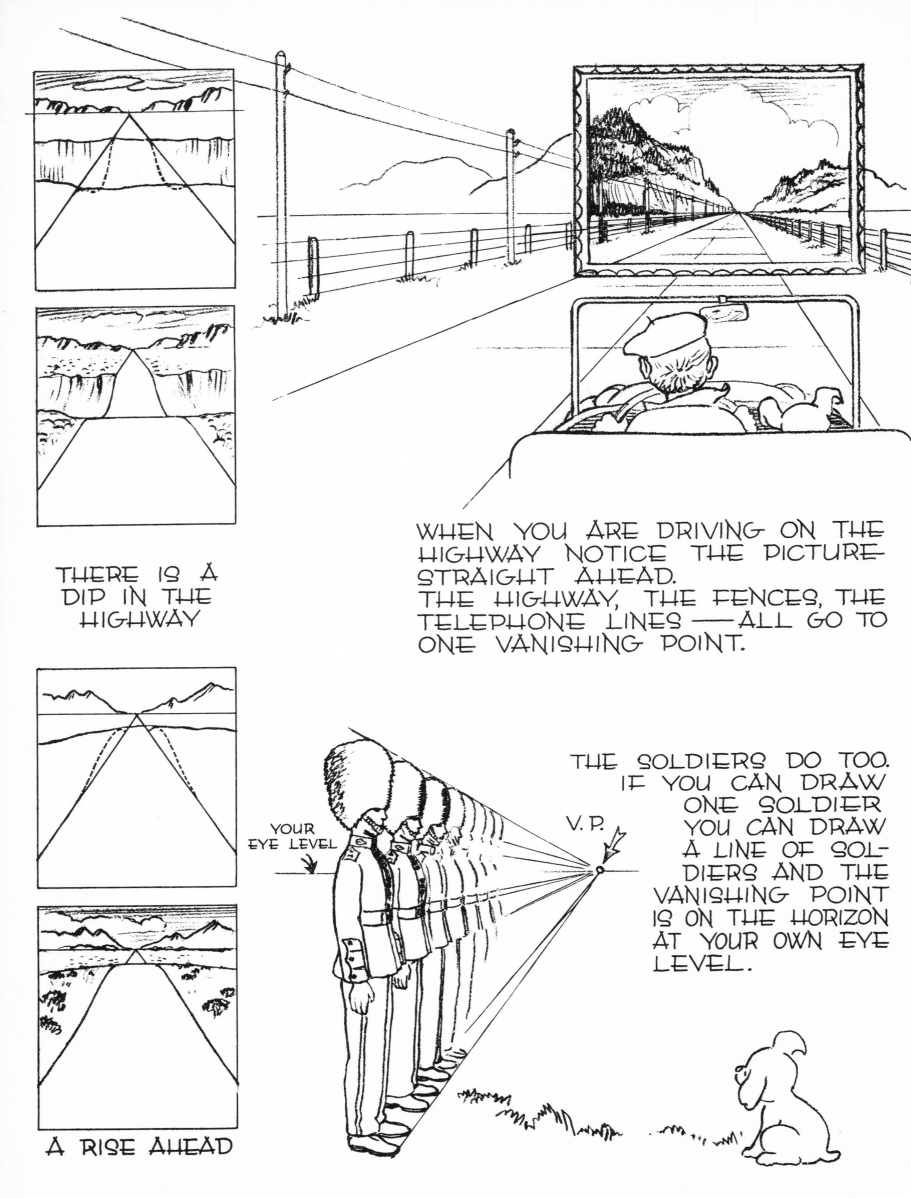

THERE IS A
DIP IN THE
HIGHWAY

WHEN YOU ARE DRIVING ON THE
HIGHWAY NOTICE THE PICTURE
STRAIGHT AHEAD.
THE HIGHWAY, THE FENCES, THE
TELEPHONE LINES — ALL GO TO
ONE VANISHING POINT.

A RISE AHEAD

YOUR
EYE LEVEL

V. P.

THE SOLDIERS DO TOO.
IF YOU CAN DRAW
ONE SOLDIER
YOU CAN DRAW
A LINE OF SOL-
DIERS AND THE
VANISHING POINT
IS ON THE HORIZON
AT YOUR OWN EYE
LEVEL.

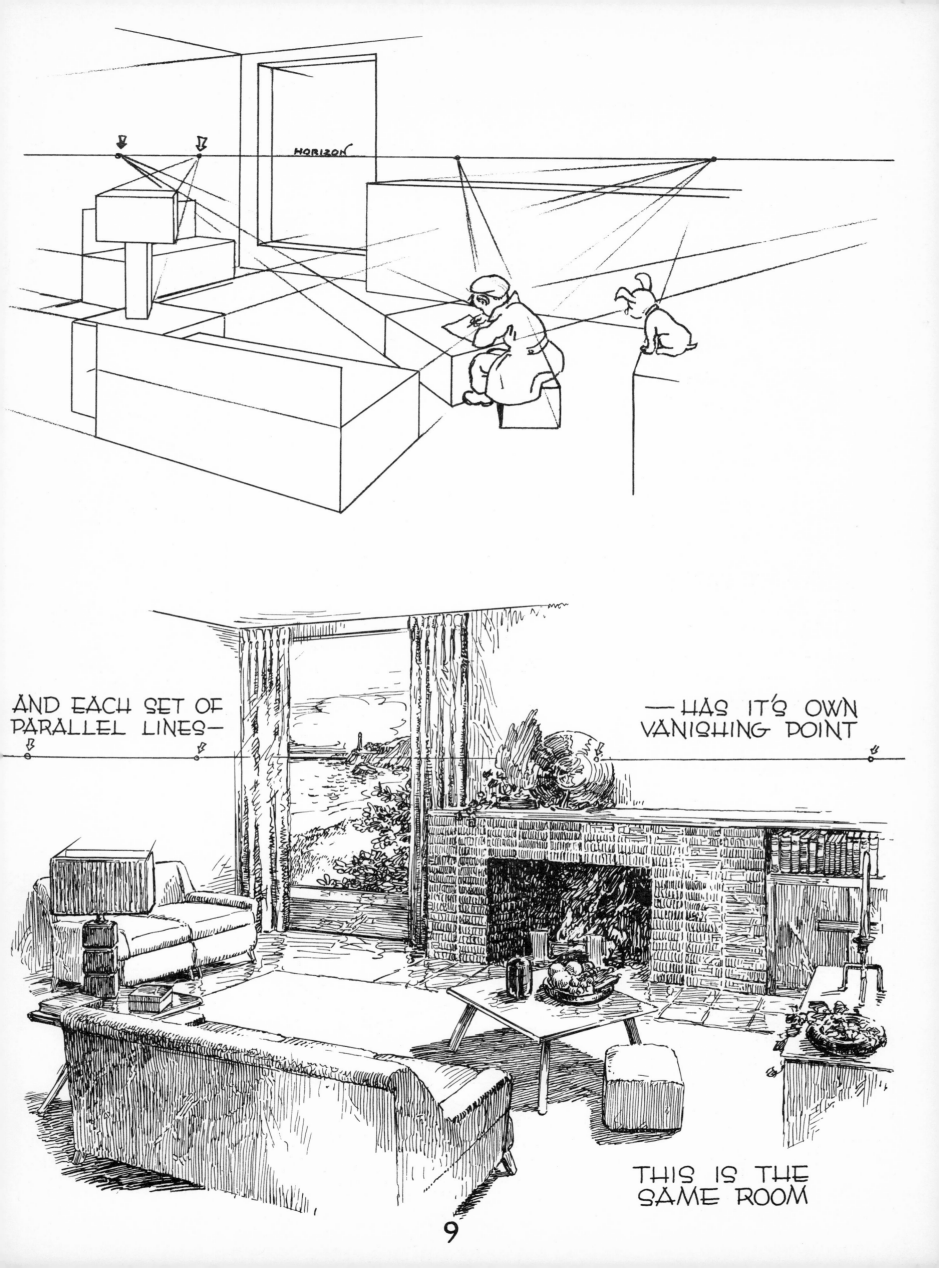

HORIZON

AND EACH SET OF
PARALLEL LINES—

—HAS IT'S OWN
VANISHING POINT

THIS IS THE
SAME ROOM

9

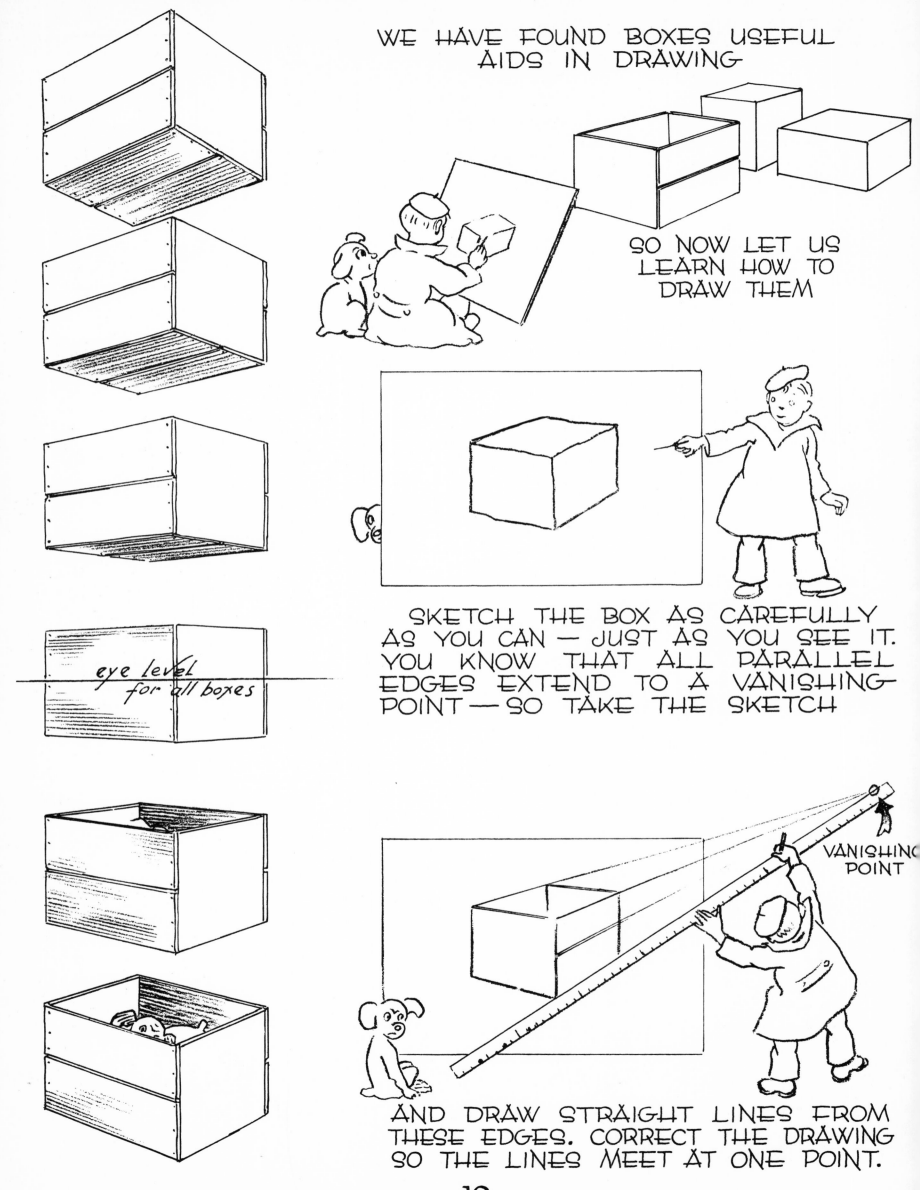

WE HAVE FOUND BOXES USEFUL
AIDS IN DRAWING

SO NOW LET US
LEARN HOW TO
DRAW THEM

*eye level
for all boxes*

SKETCH THE BOX AS CAREFULLY
AS YOU CAN — JUST AS YOU SEE IT.
YOU KNOW THAT ALL PARALLEL
EDGES EXTEND TO A VANISHING
POINT — SO TAKE THE SKETCH

VANISHING
POINT

AND DRAW STRAIGHT LINES FROM
THESE EDGES. CORRECT THE DRAWING
SO THE LINES MEET AT ONE POINT.

AFTER ONE OF THE VANISHING
POINTS HAS BEEN FOUND, THE
REST IS EASY.

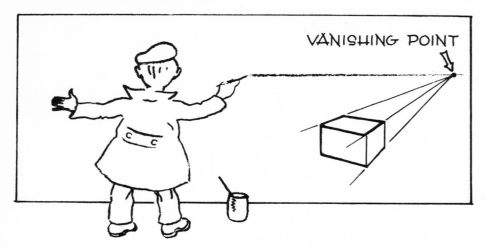

A SNAPSHOT OR A
PICTURE FROM A
MAGAZINE

THE HORIZON MUST BE LEVEL
AND IT MUST PASS THROUGH
THAT POINT.
SO DRAW THE HORIZON LINE
THROUGH THE POINT AND ACROSS
THE PAPER.

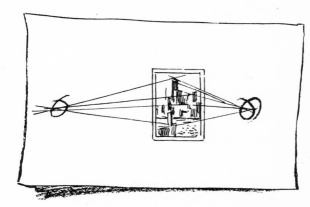

PASTE IT ON A LARGE
SHEET OF PAPER—
EXTEND THE
PERSPECTIVE LINES
THE TWO POINTS AND
THE HORIZON CAN BE
LOCATED.

THE OTHER PARALLEL LINES OF
THE BOX CAN NOW BE EXTENDED.
THEY SHOULD MEET ON THIS LINE.
THIS GIVES US THE OTHER
VANISHING POINT FOR THE BOX.

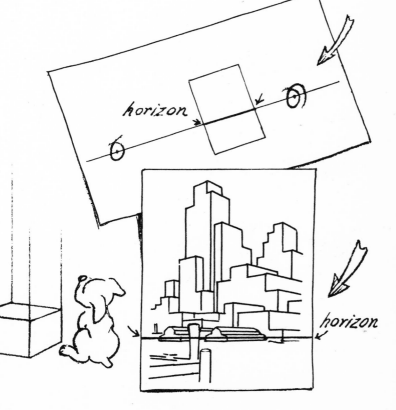

THE PERPENDICULAR LINES
DO NOT COME TOGETHER.
THEY HAVE NO VANISHING
POINT.

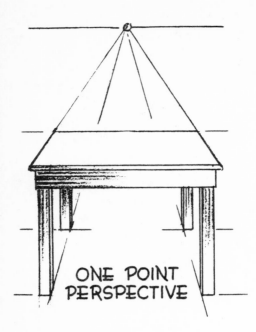

ONE POINT PERSPECTIVE

TABLES ARE SEEN WITH THE EYE-LEVEL ABOVE

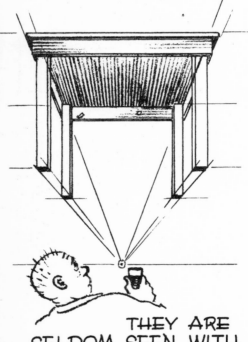

THEY ARE SELDOM SEEN WITH THE EYE-LEVEL BELOW

SMALL CHILDREN SEE THEM AT EYE-LEVEL

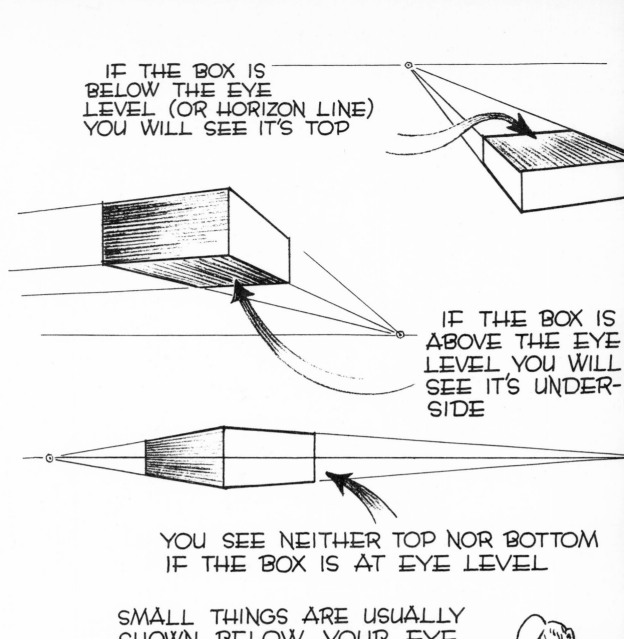

IF THE BOX IS BELOW THE EYE LEVEL (OR HORIZON LINE) YOU WILL SEE IT'S TOP

IF THE BOX IS ABOVE THE EYE LEVEL YOU WILL SEE IT'S UNDER-SIDE

YOU SEE NEITHER TOP NOR BOTTOM IF THE BOX IS AT EYE LEVEL

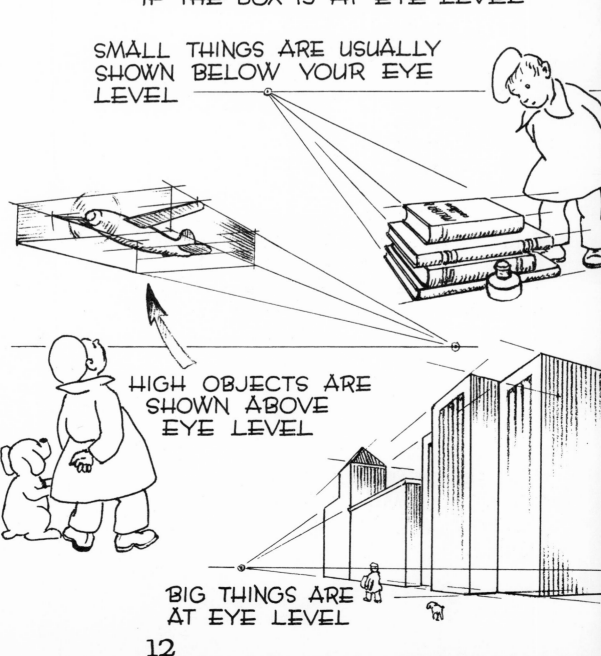

SMALL THINGS ARE USUALLY SHOWN BELOW YOUR EYE LEVEL

HIGH OBJECTS ARE SHOWN ABOVE EYE LEVEL

BIG THINGS ARE AT EYE LEVEL

HIGH THINGS AS SEEN ABOVE THE EYE LEVEL

ABOVE

EYE LEVEL

BELOW

BIG THINGS AT EYE LEVEL

ABOVE

EYE LEVEL

BELOW

SMALL THINGS AS SEEN BELOW EYE LEVEL

ROUND CANS COME IN SQUARE BOXES

13

YOU CAN MAKE A PERSPECTIVE
DRAWING OF YOUR OWN ROOM

FIRST DRAW
AN OPEN BOX, WITH
TWO VANISHING POINTS
....EYE LEVEL

NEXT REMOVE THE SIDES NEAREST TO
YOU — THIS LEAVES A CORNER IN YOUR
ROOM. (LET US DRAW IT LARGER)

FOR FURNITURE ADD
BOXES WITH VANISHING
POINTS AT EYE
LEVEL

EYE-LEVEL

EYE-LEVEL

EYE-LEVEL

AND HERE
IS THE
ROOM

YOU CAN MAKE A PERSPECTIVE DRAWING ON A WINDOW PANE WITH A GREASE PENCIL BY LOOKING THROUGH A HOLE AND TRACING WHAT YOU SEE.
THE HOLE IS YOUR "EYE LEVEL" AND IT IS THE SAME HEIGHT AS THE "HORIZON LINE."

THE WINDOW PANE IS THE "PICTURE PLANE" AND THE SPOT ON THE FLOOR BELOW YOU IS YOUR "STATION POINT."

EYE LEVEL, PICTURE PLANE AND OBJECT

HEIGHT OF EYE

STATION POINT ON THE FLOOR

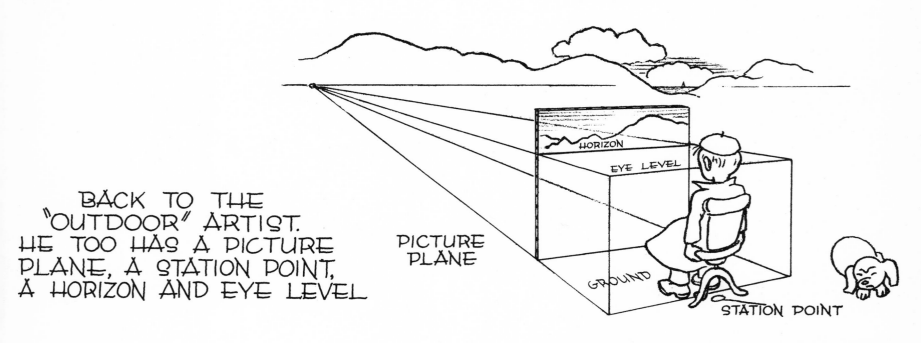

BACK TO THE "OUTDOOR" ARTIST. HE TOO HAS A PICTURE PLANE, A STATION POINT, A HORIZON AND EYE LEVEL

PICTURE PLANE

HORIZON

EYE LEVEL

GROUND

STATION POINT

THE VANISHING POINTS ARE SOMEWHERE ON THE HORIZON LINE – BUT WHERE?

15

LOCATING THE VANISHING POINTS

HERE IS THE ARTIST AGAIN DRAWING A BOX

WE ARE LOOKING STRAIGHT DOWN ON HIM. HE IS STANDING ON HIS STATION POINT AND HE IS DRAWING ON A TRANSPARENT PICTURE PLANE. WE ARE LOOKING DOWN ON IT'S TOP EDGE.

NOW IN ORDER TO FIND A VANISHING POINT ON HIS HORIZON LINE HE WILL HAVE TO LOOK IN THE DIRECTION PARALLEL TO THE SIDES OF THE BOX.

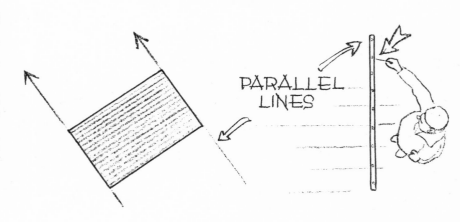

PARALLEL LINES

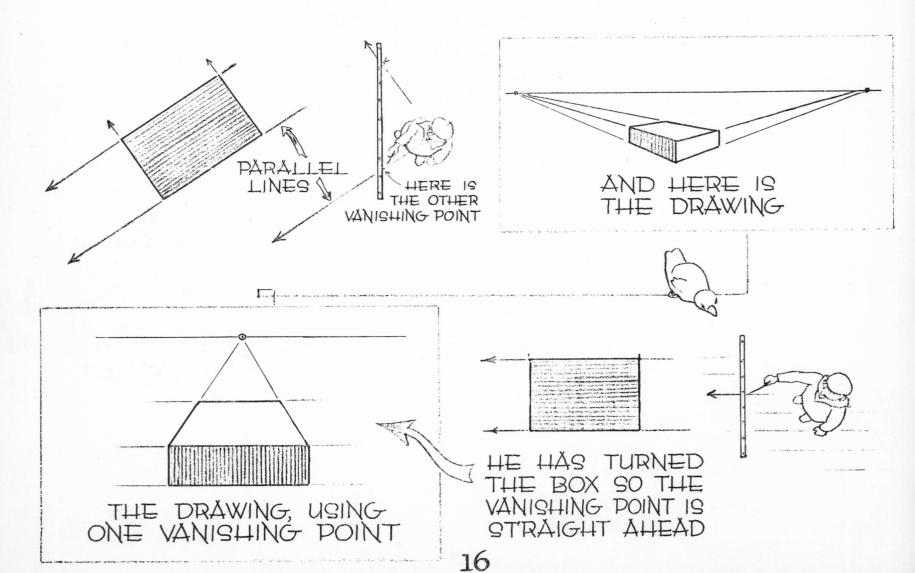

PARALLEL LINES

HERE IS THE OTHER VANISHING POINT

AND HERE IS THE DRAWING

THE DRAWING, USING ONE VANISHING POINT

HE HAS TURNED THE BOX SO THE VANISHING POINT IS STRAIGHT AHEAD

16

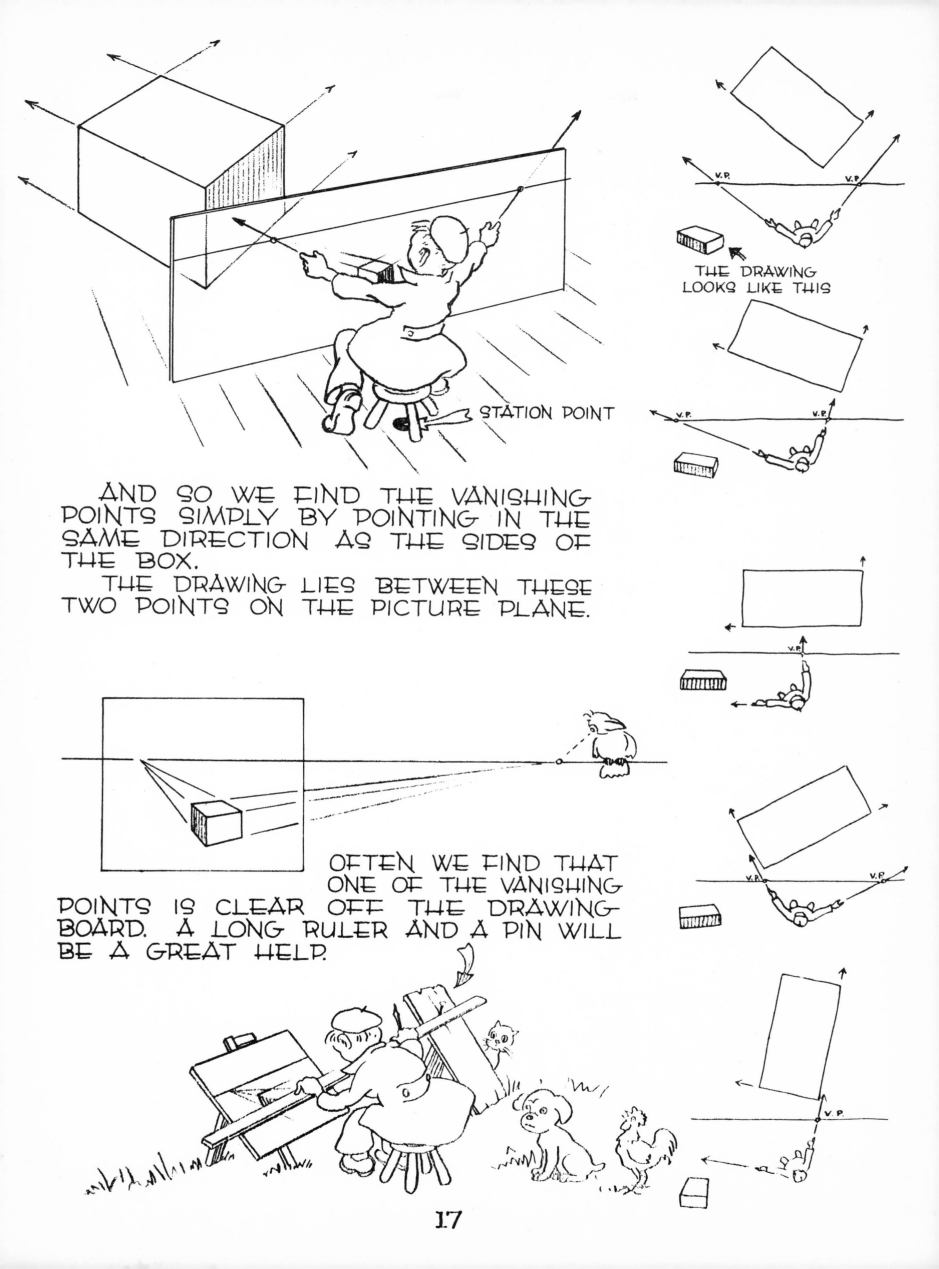

STATION POINT

THE DRAWING
LOOKS LIKE THIS

AND SO WE FIND THE VANISHING
POINTS SIMPLY BY POINTING IN THE
SAME DIRECTION AS THE SIDES OF
THE BOX.

THE DRAWING LIES BETWEEN THESE
TWO POINTS ON THE PICTURE PLANE.

OFTEN WE FIND THAT
ONE OF THE VANISHING
POINTS IS CLEAR OFF THE DRAWING
BOARD. A LONG RULER AND A PIN WILL
BE A GREAT HELP.

VANISHING POINTS
SHOULD BE PLACED FAR APART——LIKE THIS

GOOD SPACING

SPACING WITH VANISHING
POINTS TOO CLOSE

O.K.

O.K.

No!   No!

THIS WAY ——— AND NOT THIS WAY

WIDE SPACING MAKES GOOD DRAWING

TOO CLOSE

CLOSE SPACING
THE AIRPLANE LOOKS LOP-SIDED
AND POORLY DRAWN.

WE ARE READY TO MAKE A TRUE PERSPECTIVE DRAWING

THIS IS THE TOP VIEW (THE PLAN) OF A BOX.

THIS IS THE SIDE VIEW (THE SIDE ELEVATION) OF THE SAME BOX.

WE WISH TO MAKE A DRAWING OF THE BOX— LOOKING AT IT CORNERWISE.

SO WE STAND AWAY FROM IT AT ANY DISTANCE WE PLEASE AND MAKE A DOT AT OUR STATION POINT.

A SQUARE CORNER (90°)

NOW WE DRAW THE LINE WHICH REPRESENTS THE PICTURE PLANE RESTING UPRIGHT AGAINST THE CORNER OF THE PLAN LIKE THIS!

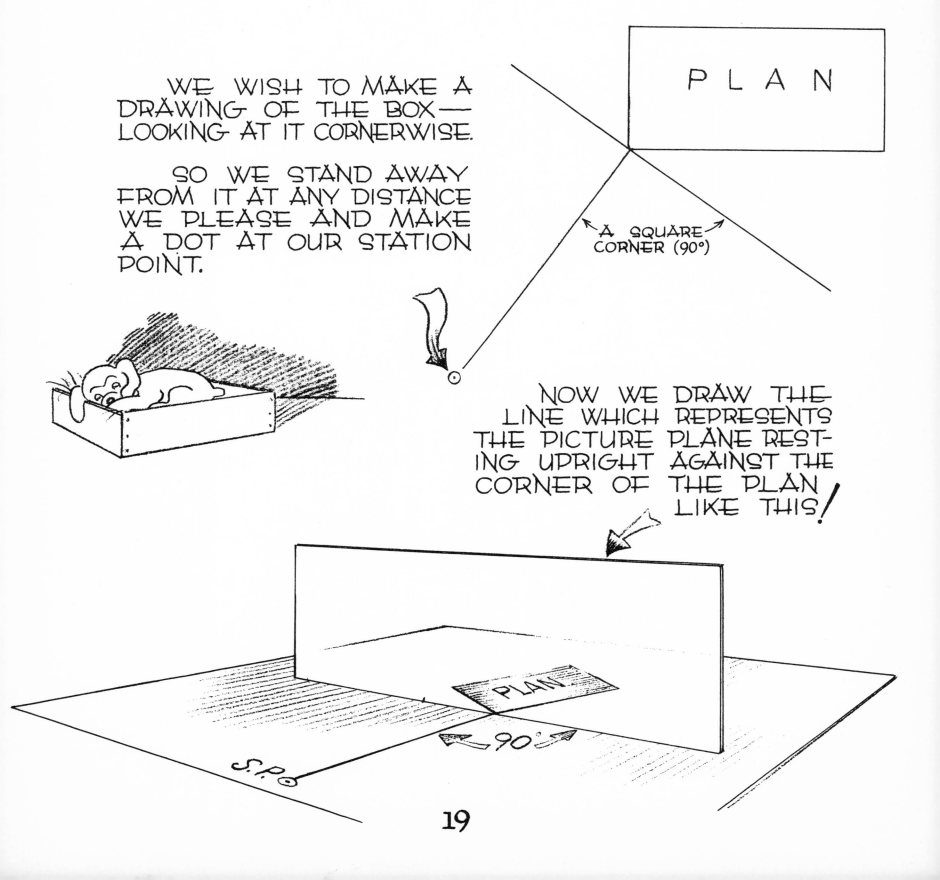

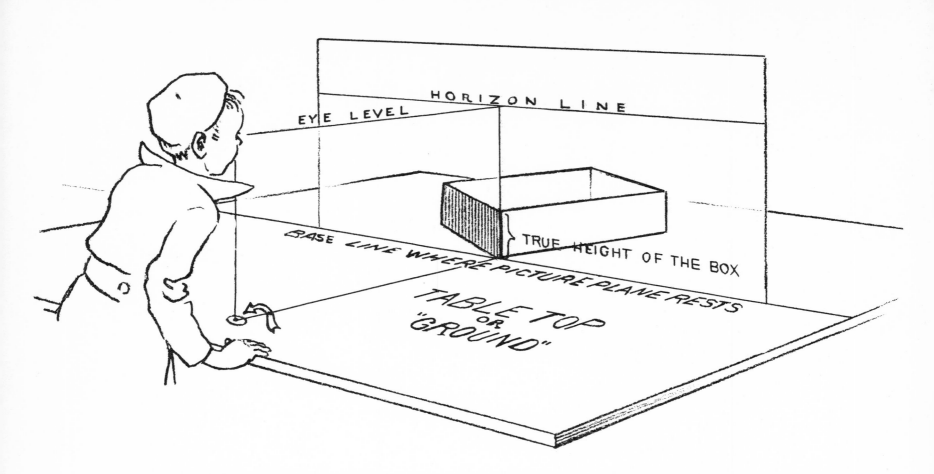

IF THE BOX COULD BE PLACED ON THE PLAN IT WOULD LOOK LIKE THIS.

WE WOULD LOOK AT IT FROM A POSITION DIRECTLY ABOVE THE STATION POINT AT ANY CONVENIENT HEIGHT. (THE HEAVY BLACK LINE AT THE CORNER OF THE BOX IS ITS TRUE HEIGHT ON THE PICTURE PLANE.)

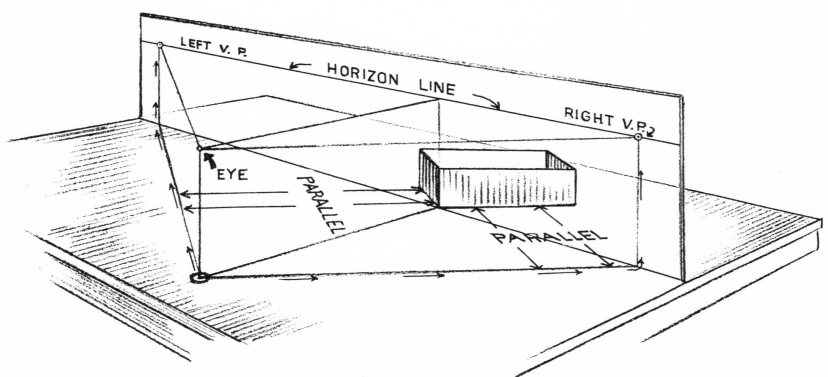

WE LOCATE THE VANISHING POINTS BY RUNNING LINES FROM THE EYE TO THE PICTURE PLANE, PARALLEL TO THE SIDES OF THE BOX.

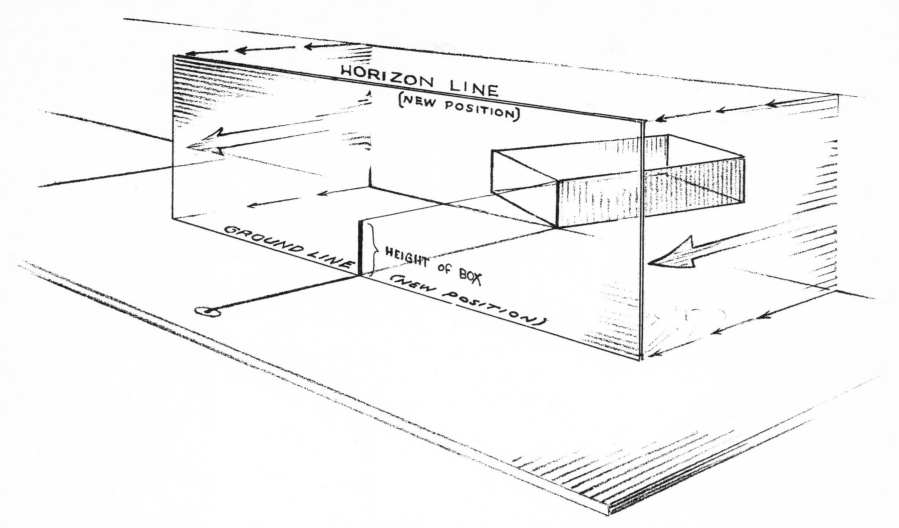

WE ARE MAKING THE DRAWING ON THE PICTURE PLANE.
WE WANT IT FOR CONVENIENCE TO LIE FLAT ON THE
TABLE TOP, OR GROUND.   TO DO THIS WE SLIDE IT——
AS SHOWN————TOWARDS US INTO THE OPEN SPACE
BETWEEN THE STATION POINT AND THE PLAN.

VANISHING POINTS COME FORWARD TOO.

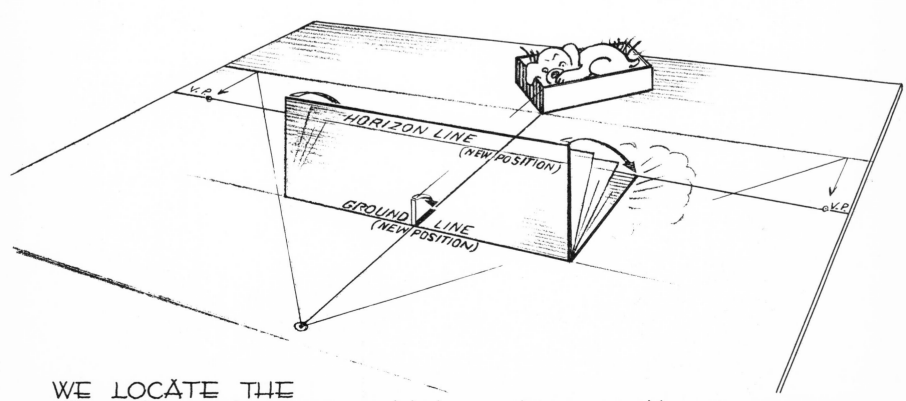

WE LOCATE THE
VANISHING POINTS BY RUNNING LINES FROM THE EYE TO
THE PICTURE PLANE, PARALLEL TO THE SIDES OF THE BOX.

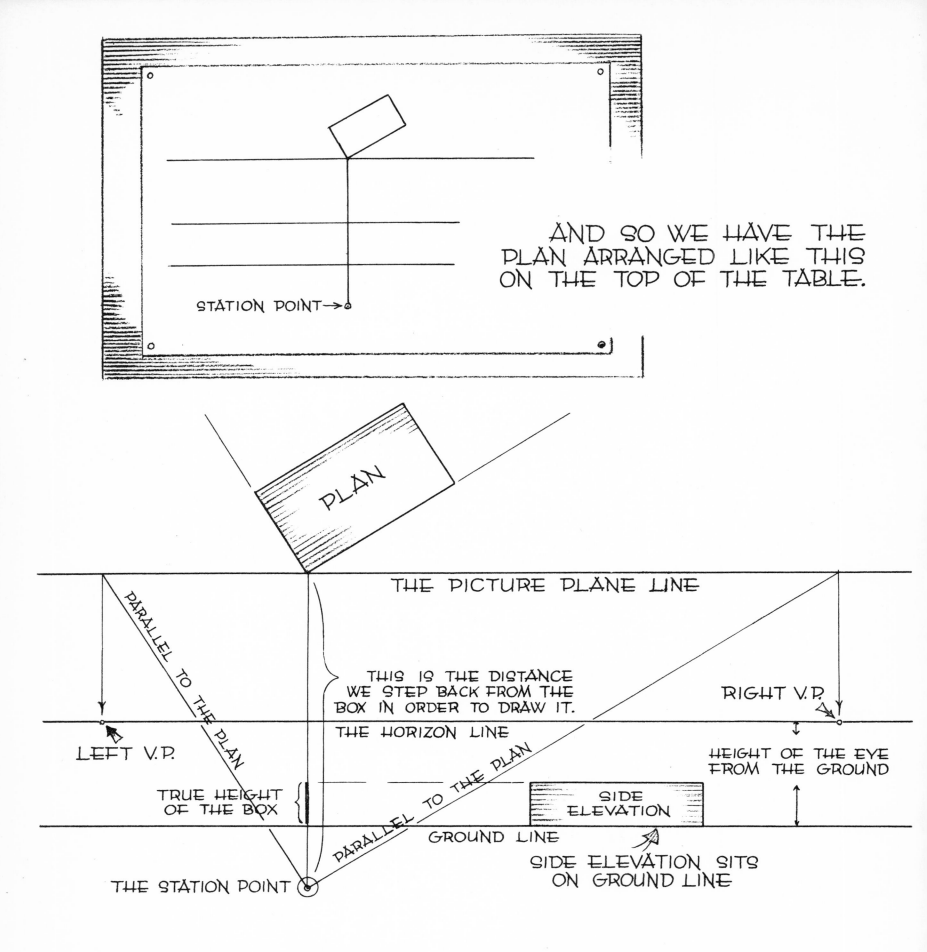

STATION POINT →

AND SO WE HAVE THE PLAN ARRANGED LIKE THIS ON THE TOP OF THE TABLE.

PLAN

THE PICTURE PLANE LINE

PARALLEL TO THE PLAN

THIS IS THE DISTANCE WE STEP BACK FROM THE BOX IN ORDER TO DRAW IT.

RIGHT V.P.

THE HORIZON LINE

LEFT V.P.

HEIGHT OF THE EYE FROM THE GROUND

TRUE HEIGHT OF THE BOX

PARALLEL TO THE PLAN

SIDE ELEVATION

GROUND LINE

SIDE ELEVATION SITS ON GROUND LINE

THE STATION POINT

HERE IS THE TYPICAL PERSPECTIVE PLAN WITH THE PARTS NAMED.

NOTICE THAT THE VANISHING POINTS ARE TRANSFERRED TO THE HORIZON LINE WHICH IS NOW LYING ON THE GROUND. THEIR DISTANCE APART REMAINS UNCHANGED.

THE DRAWING OF THE SIDE ELEVATION IS PLACED ON THE GROUND LINE. HERE IT IS USED FOR THE UP AND DOWN OR HEIGHT MEASUREMENTS.

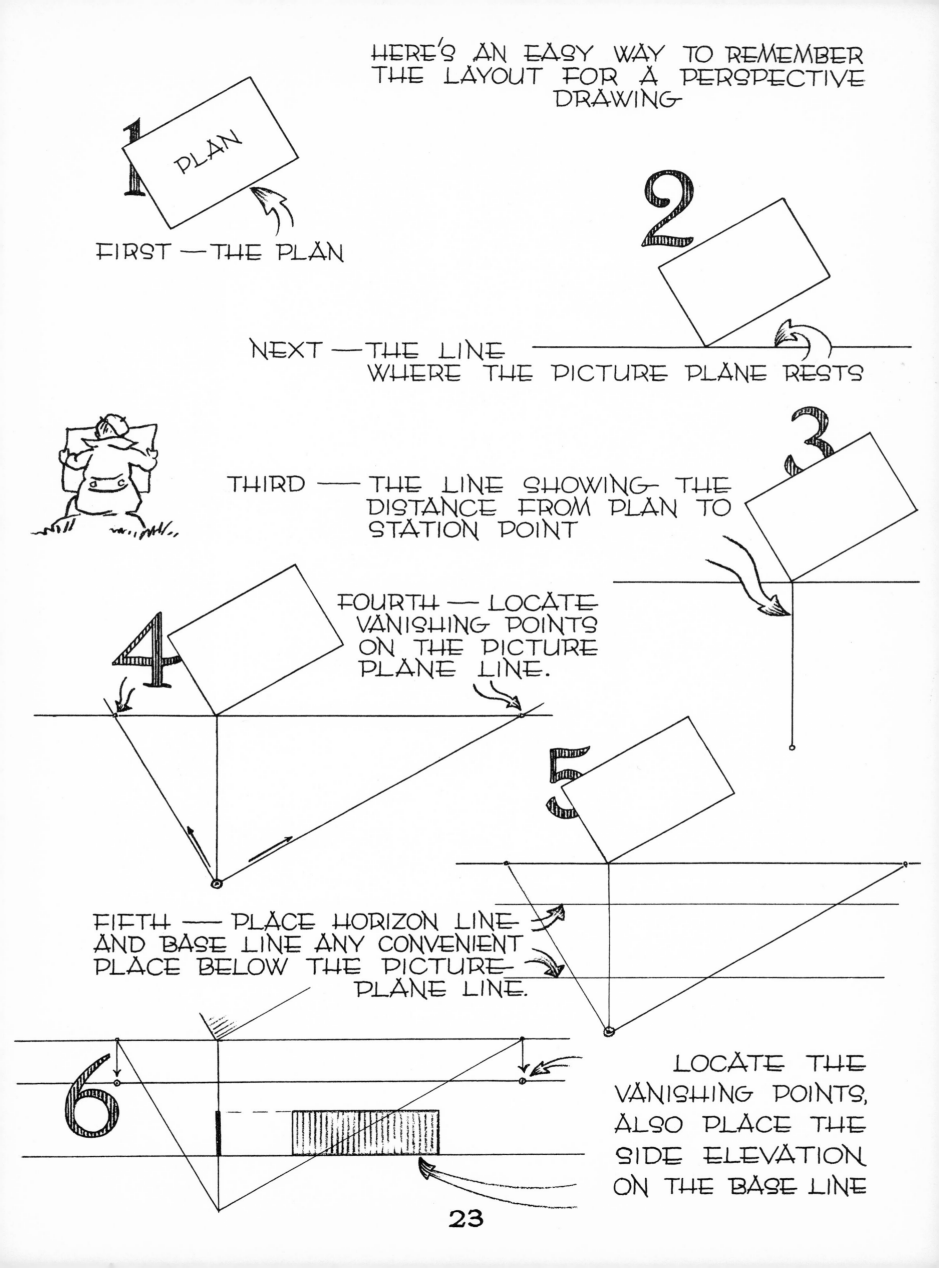

HERE'S AN EASY WAY TO REMEMBER THE LAYOUT FOR A PERSPECTIVE DRAWING

1 PLAN

FIRST — THE PLAN

2

NEXT — THE LINE WHERE THE PICTURE PLANE RESTS

3

THIRD — THE LINE SHOWING THE DISTANCE FROM PLAN TO STATION POINT

4 FOURTH — LOCATE VANISHING POINTS ON THE PICTURE PLANE LINE.

5

FIFTH — PLACE HORIZON LINE AND BASE LINE ANY CONVENIENT PLACE BELOW THE PICTURE PLANE LINE.

6 LOCATE THE VANISHING POINTS, ALSO PLACE THE SIDE ELEVATION ON THE BASE LINE

23

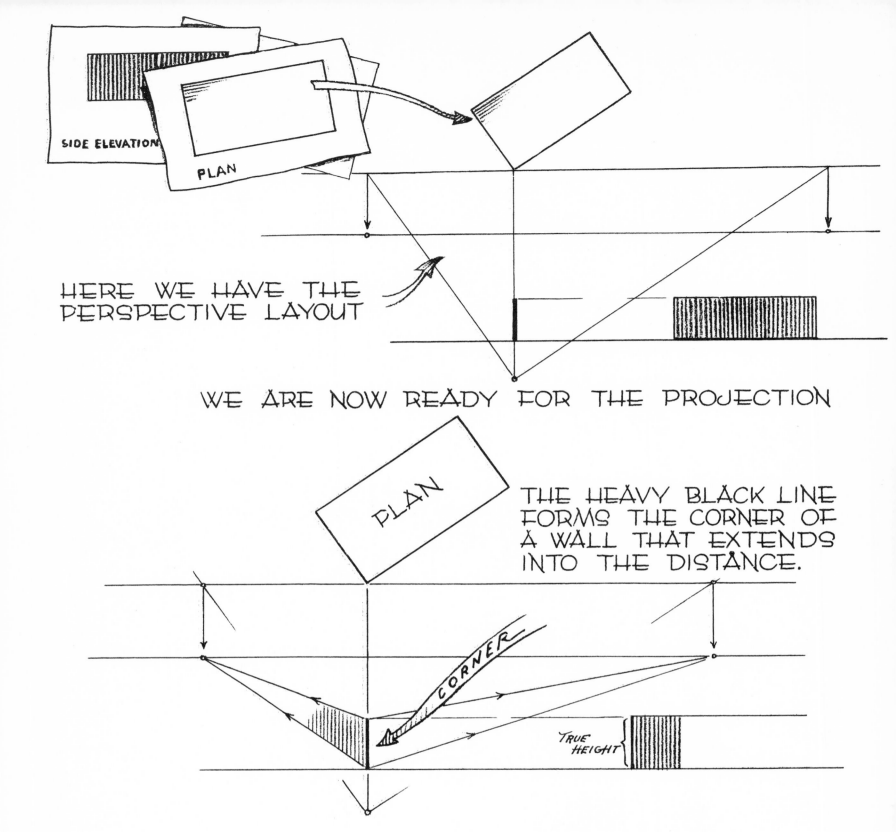

SIDE ELEVATION

PLAN

HERE WE HAVE THE
PERSPECTIVE LAYOUT

WE ARE NOW READY FOR THE PROJECTION

PLAN

THE HEAVY BLACK LINE
FORMS THE CORNER OF
A WALL THAT EXTENDS
INTO THE DISTANCE.

CORNER

TRUE
HEIGHT

THE WALL, LIKE THE RAILROAD TRACK, DISAPPEARS
AT THE VANISHING POINTS ON THE HORIZON.
THE WALL IS THE HEIGHT OF THE BOX; — IT IS
MADE BY DRAWING FOUR LINES FROM THE TOP AND
BOTTOM OF THE HEAVY LINE OUT TO THE VANISHING
POINTS, NOW ALL WE HAVE TO DO IS TO CUT THE
TWO WALLS OFF AT THE PROPER LENGTH SO AS TO
MAKE TWO SIDES OF THE BOX.

LET'S SEE HOW IT'S DONE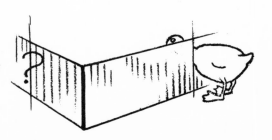

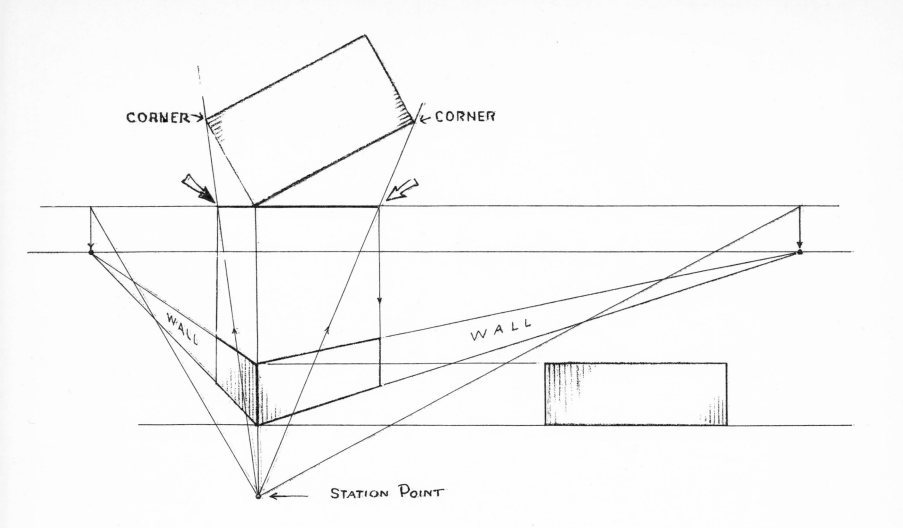

WE ARE STANDING AT THE STATION POINT LOOKING AT THE PLAN. FROM HERE WE LOOK ALONG A STRAIGHT LINE TO A POINT AT THE CORNER OF THE PLAN. THIS LINE PASSES THROUGH THE PICTURE PLANE AT THE POINT INDICATED BY THE ARROW. THERE ARE TWO OF THESE POINTS, ONE FOR EACH CORNER.

NOW THE BOX AS WE SEE IT ON THE PICTURE PLANE LIES IN THE SPACE BETWEEN THE ARROWS. IT IS NO WIDER THAN THIS SPACE. SO LINES FROM THE POINTS, DRAWN STRAIGHT DOWN, CUT THE WALLS OFF AT THE RIGHT WIDTH. WE NOW HAVE TWO SIDES OF THE BOX DRAWN IN PERSPECTIVE.

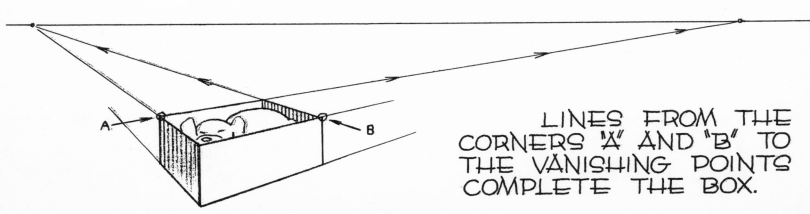

LINES FROM THE CORNERS "A" AND "B" TO THE VANISHING POINTS COMPLETE THE BOX.

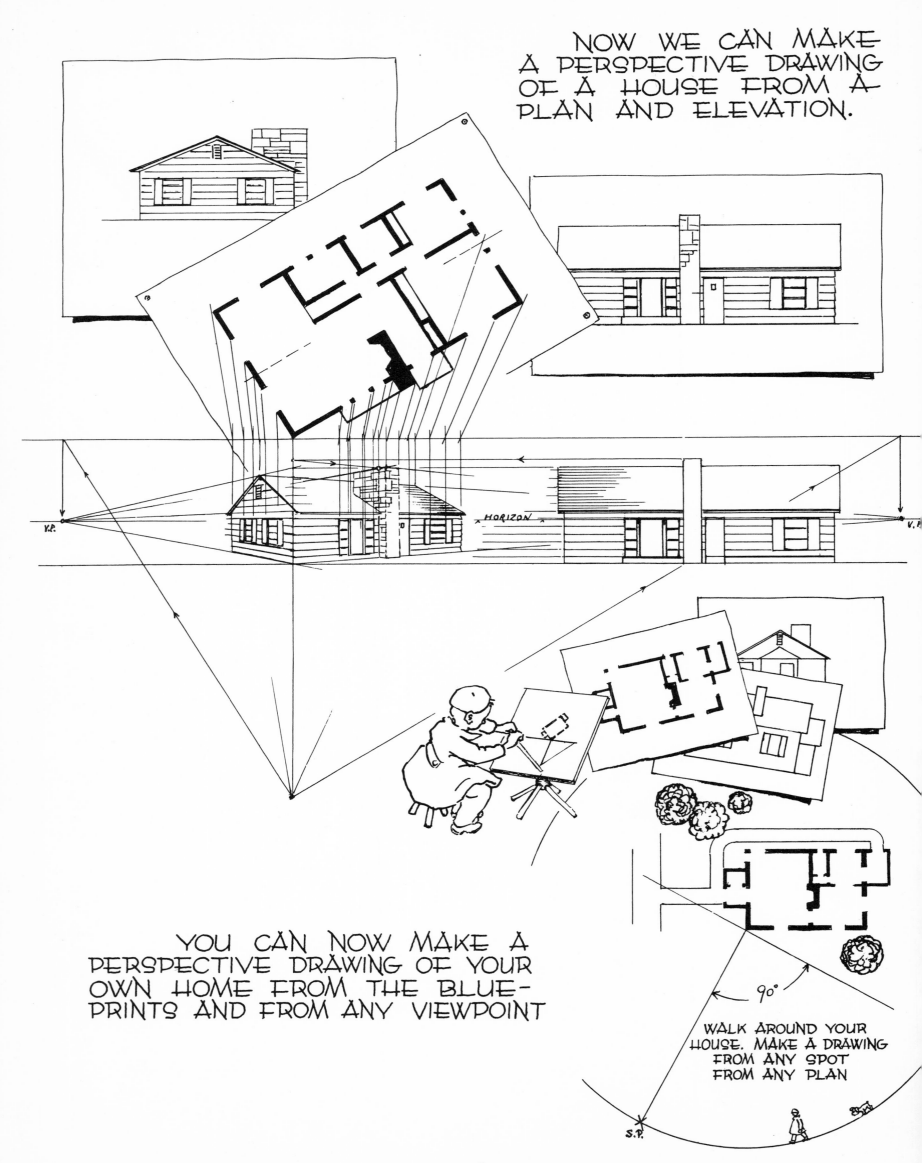

NOW WE CAN MAKE
A PERSPECTIVE DRAWING
OF A HOUSE FROM A
PLAN AND ELEVATION.

HORIZON

V.P.

V.P.

S.P.

90°

YOU CAN NOW MAKE A
PERSPECTIVE DRAWING OF YOUR
OWN HOME FROM THE BLUE-
PRINTS AND FROM ANY VIEWPOINT

WALK AROUND YOUR
HOUSE. MAKE A DRAWING
FROM ANY SPOT
FROM ANY PLAN

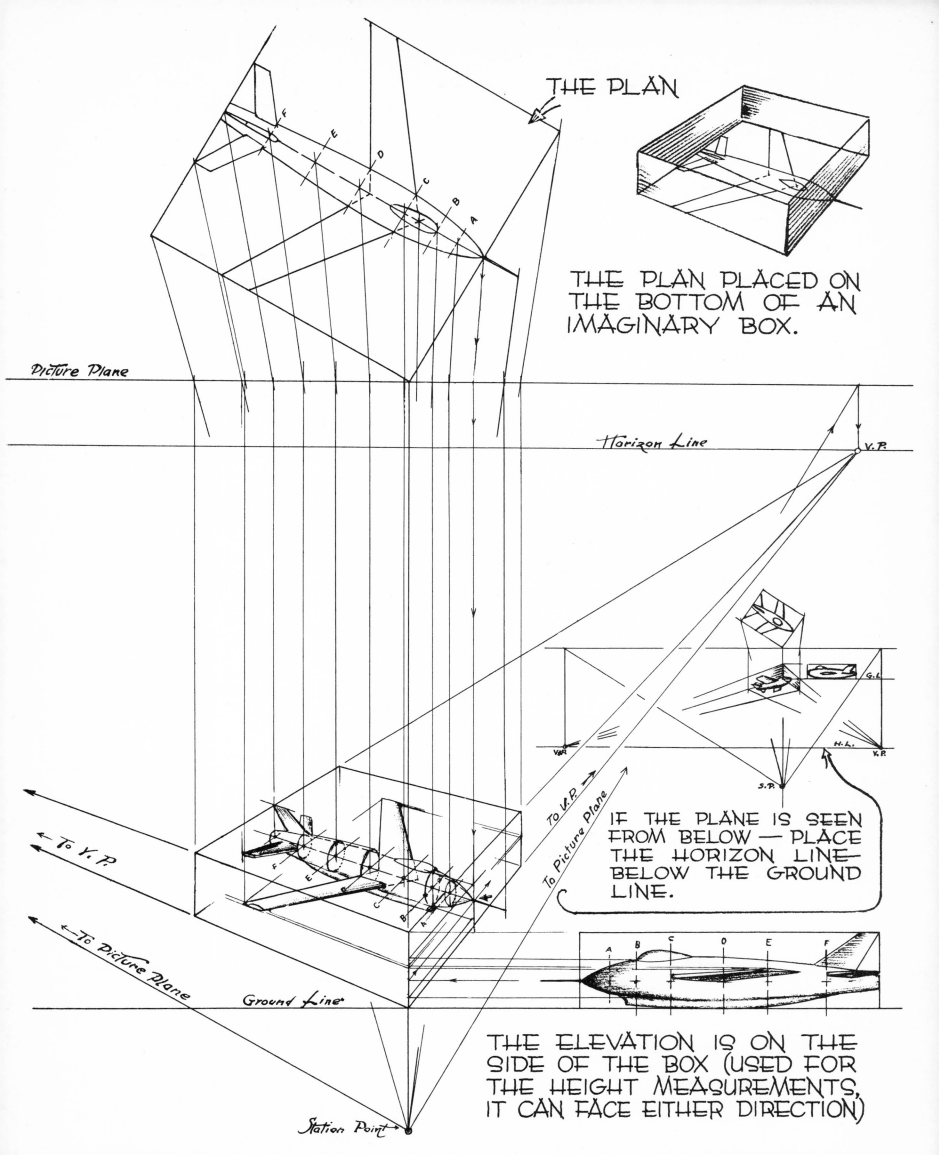

THE PLAN

THE PLAN PLACED ON THE BOTTOM OF AN IMAGINARY BOX.

Picture Plane

Horizon Line — V.P.

To V.P.

To Picture Plane

IF THE PLANE IS SEEN FROM BELOW — PLACE THE HORIZON LINE BELOW THE GROUND LINE.

To V.P.

To Picture Plane

Ground Line

Station Point

THE ELEVATION IS ON THE SIDE OF THE BOX (USED FOR THE HEIGHT MEASUREMENTS, IT CAN FACE EITHER DIRECTION)

A PERSPECTIVE PROJECTION OF A JET PLANE DRAWN FROM A PLAN AND A SIDE ELEVATION

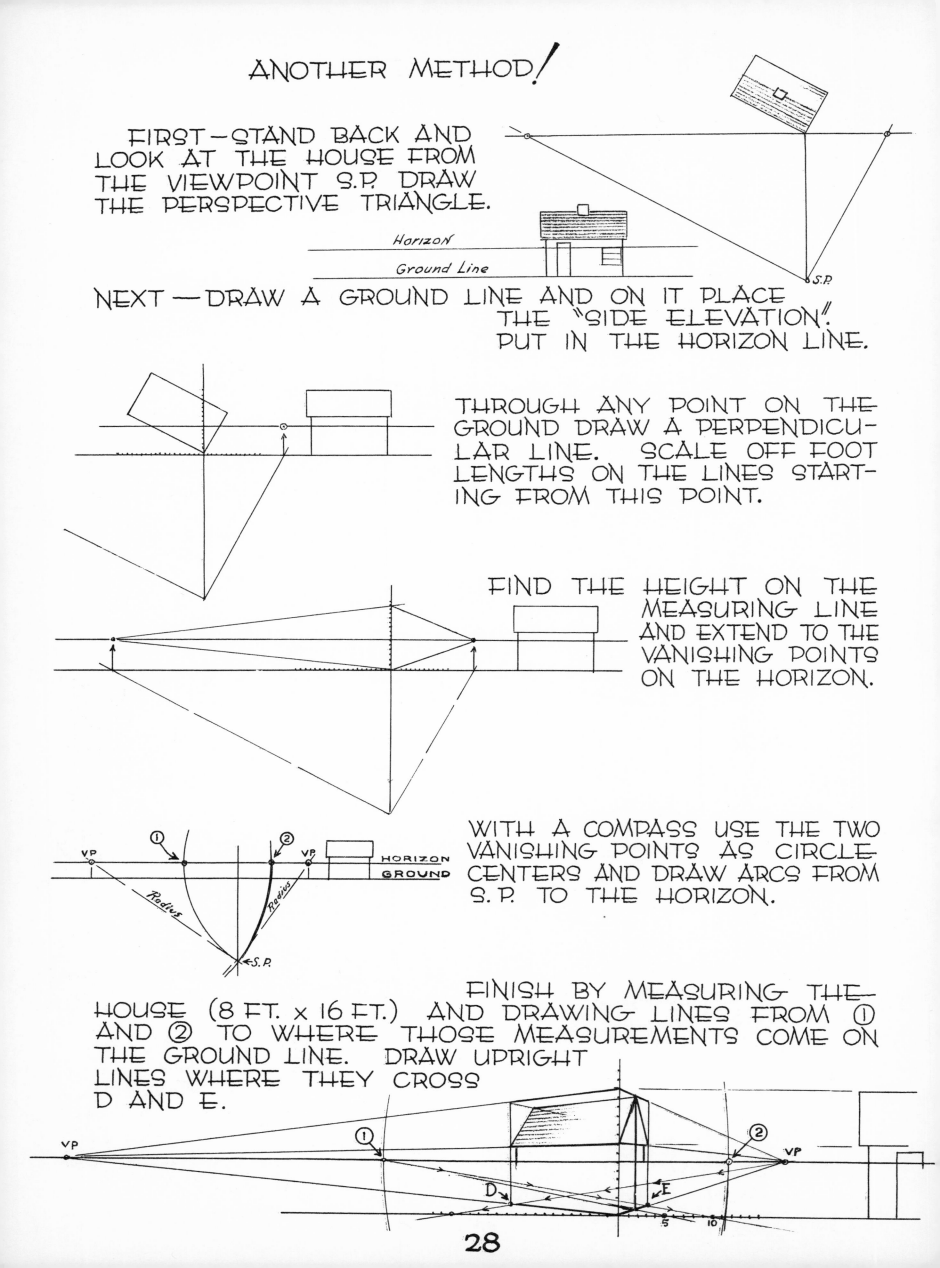

ANOTHER METHOD!

FIRST—STAND BACK AND LOOK AT THE HOUSE FROM THE VIEWPOINT S.P. DRAW THE PERSPECTIVE TRIANGLE.

Horizon

Ground Line

NEXT—DRAW A GROUND LINE AND ON IT PLACE THE "SIDE ELEVATION". PUT IN THE HORIZON LINE.

THROUGH ANY POINT ON THE GROUND DRAW A PERPENDICULAR LINE. SCALE OFF FOOT LENGTHS ON THE LINES STARTING FROM THIS POINT.

FIND THE HEIGHT ON THE MEASURING LINE AND EXTEND TO THE VANISHING POINTS ON THE HORIZON.

WITH A COMPASS USE THE TWO VANISHING POINTS AS CIRCLE CENTERS AND DRAW ARCS FROM S.P. TO THE HORIZON.

FINISH BY MEASURING THE HOUSE (8 FT. x 16 FT.) AND DRAWING LINES FROM ① AND ② TO WHERE THOSE MEASUREMENTS COME ON THE GROUND LINE. DRAW UPRIGHT LINES WHERE THEY CROSS D AND E.

THREE KINDS OF PERSPECTIVE

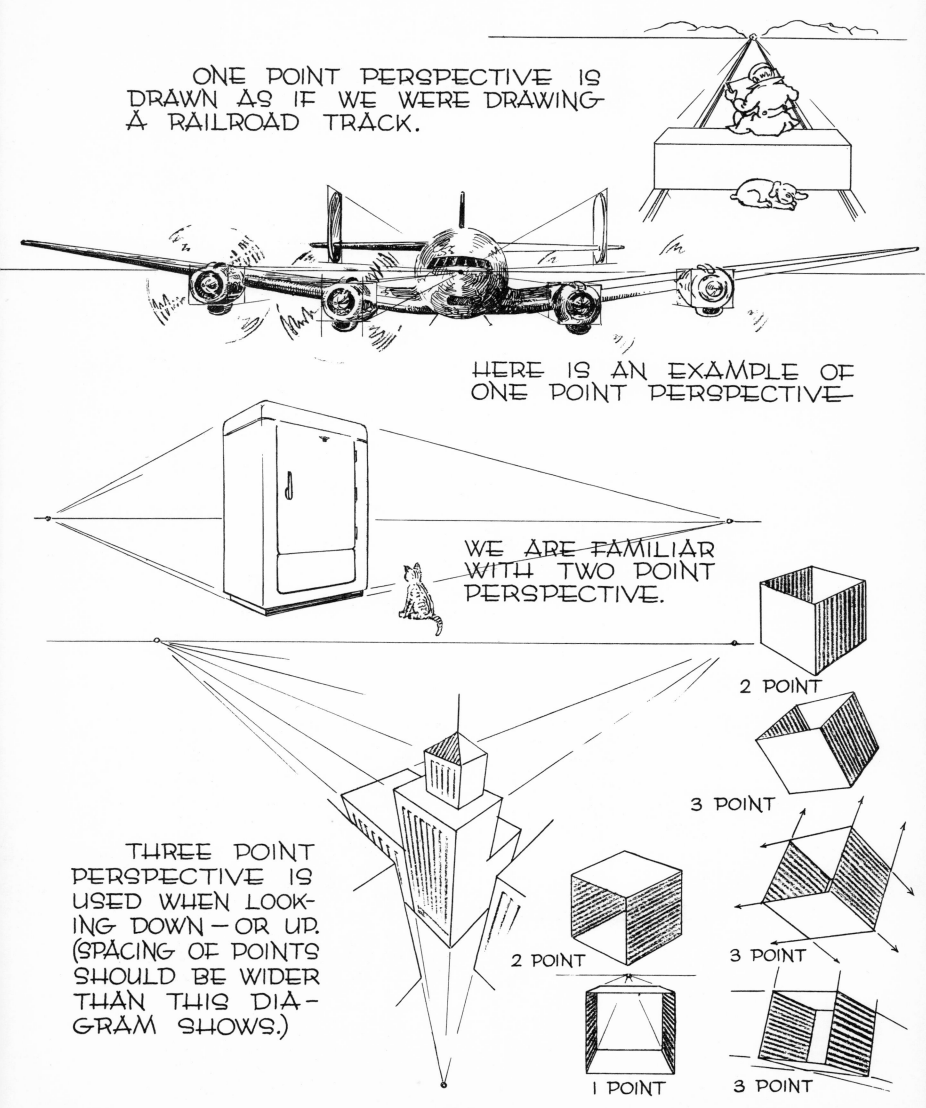

ONE POINT PERSPECTIVE IS DRAWN AS IF WE WERE DRAWING A RAILROAD TRACK.

HERE IS AN EXAMPLE OF ONE POINT PERSPECTIVE

WE ARE FAMILIAR WITH TWO POINT PERSPECTIVE.

2 POINT

3 POINT

THREE POINT PERSPECTIVE IS USED WHEN LOOKING DOWN — OR UP. (SPACING OF POINTS SHOULD BE WIDER THAN THIS DIAGRAM SHOWS.)

2 POINT

3 POINT

1 POINT

3 POINT

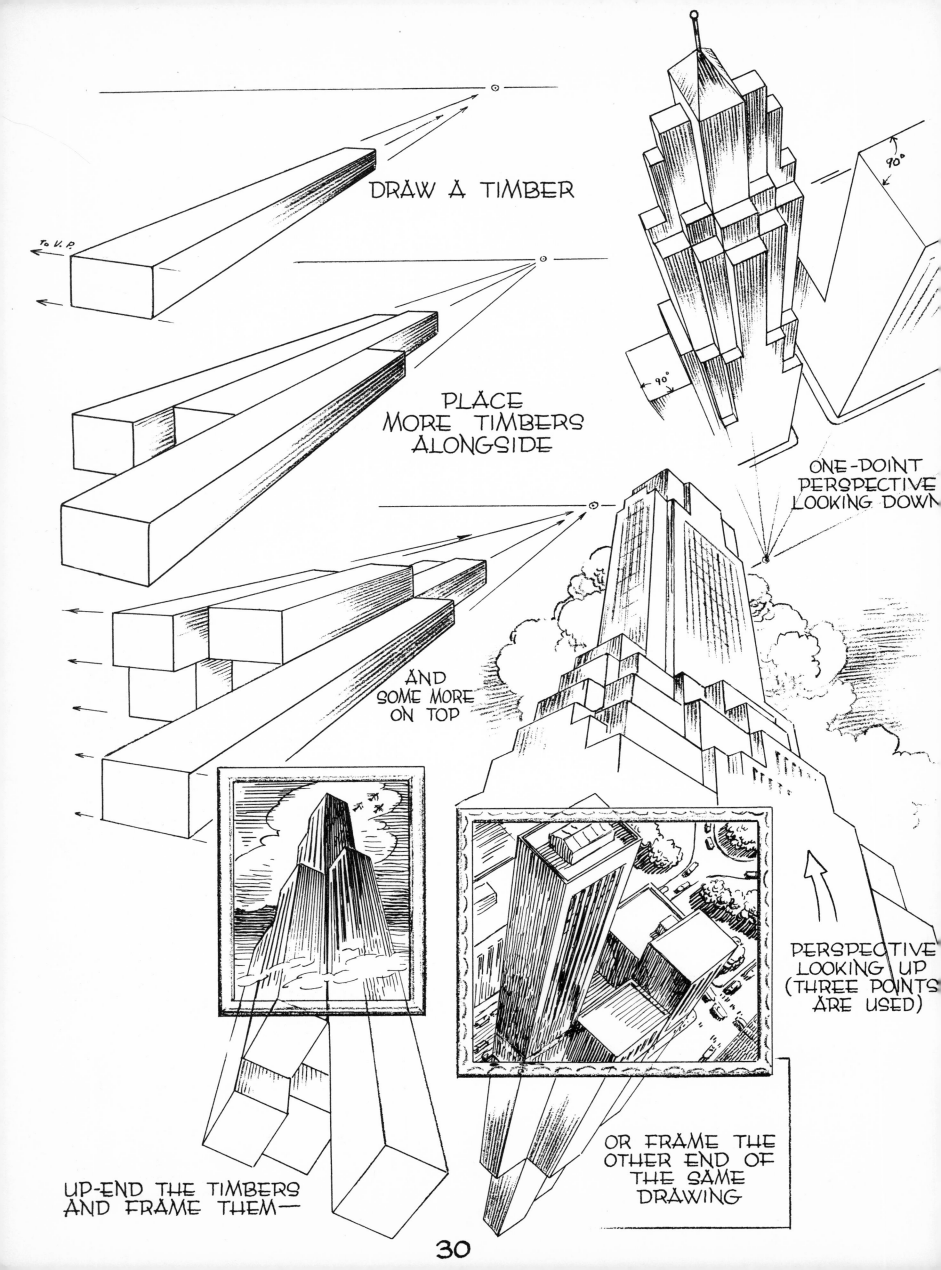

DRAW A TIMBER

To V.P.

PLACE MORE TIMBERS ALONGSIDE

AND SOME MORE ON TOP

90°

90°

ONE-POINT PERSPECTIVE LOOKING DOWN

PERSPECTIVE LOOKING UP (THREE POINTS ARE USED)

UP-END THE TIMBERS AND FRAME THEM—

OR FRAME THE OTHER END OF THE SAME DRAWING

30

THE CIRCLE IN PERSPECTIVE IS AN ELLIPSE

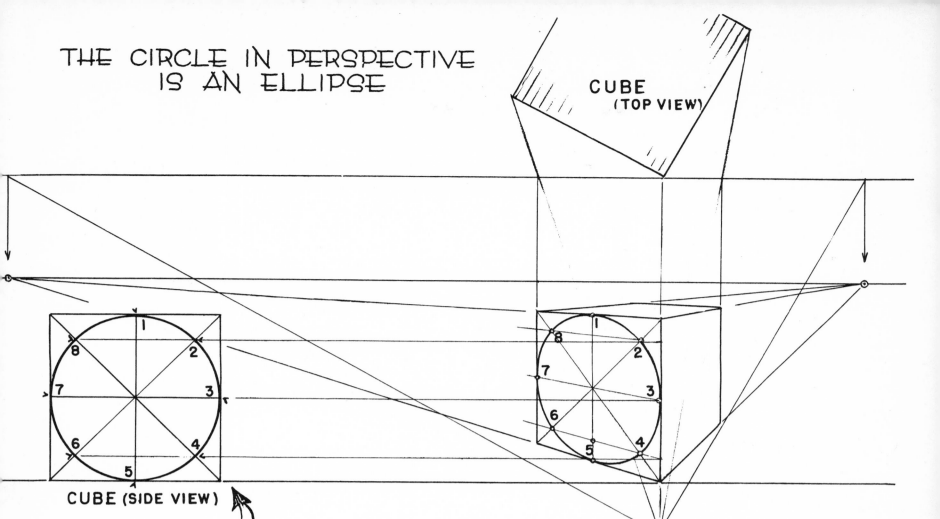

CUBE (TOP VIEW)

CUBE (SIDE VIEW)

DRAW THE DIAGONALS ON THE SIDE VIEW. THEY CROSS AT THE CENTER OF THE CIRCLE. DRAW THE CIRCLE.

CIRCLES IN A SQUARE TOUCH AT 4 POINTS

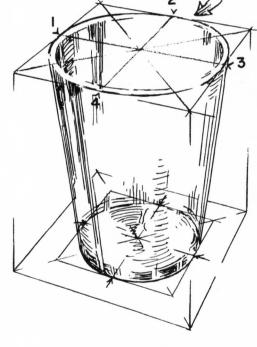

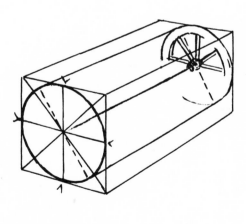

A CYLINDER IS LIKE A PAIR OF WHEELS ON AN AXEL. ALWAYS DRAW THE LONG LINE OF THE ELLIPSE — (CALLED THE MAJOR AXIS) — SO IT MAKES A RIGHT ANGLE WITH THE AXLE.

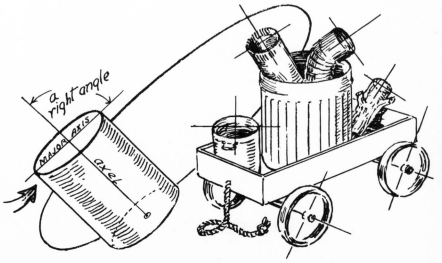

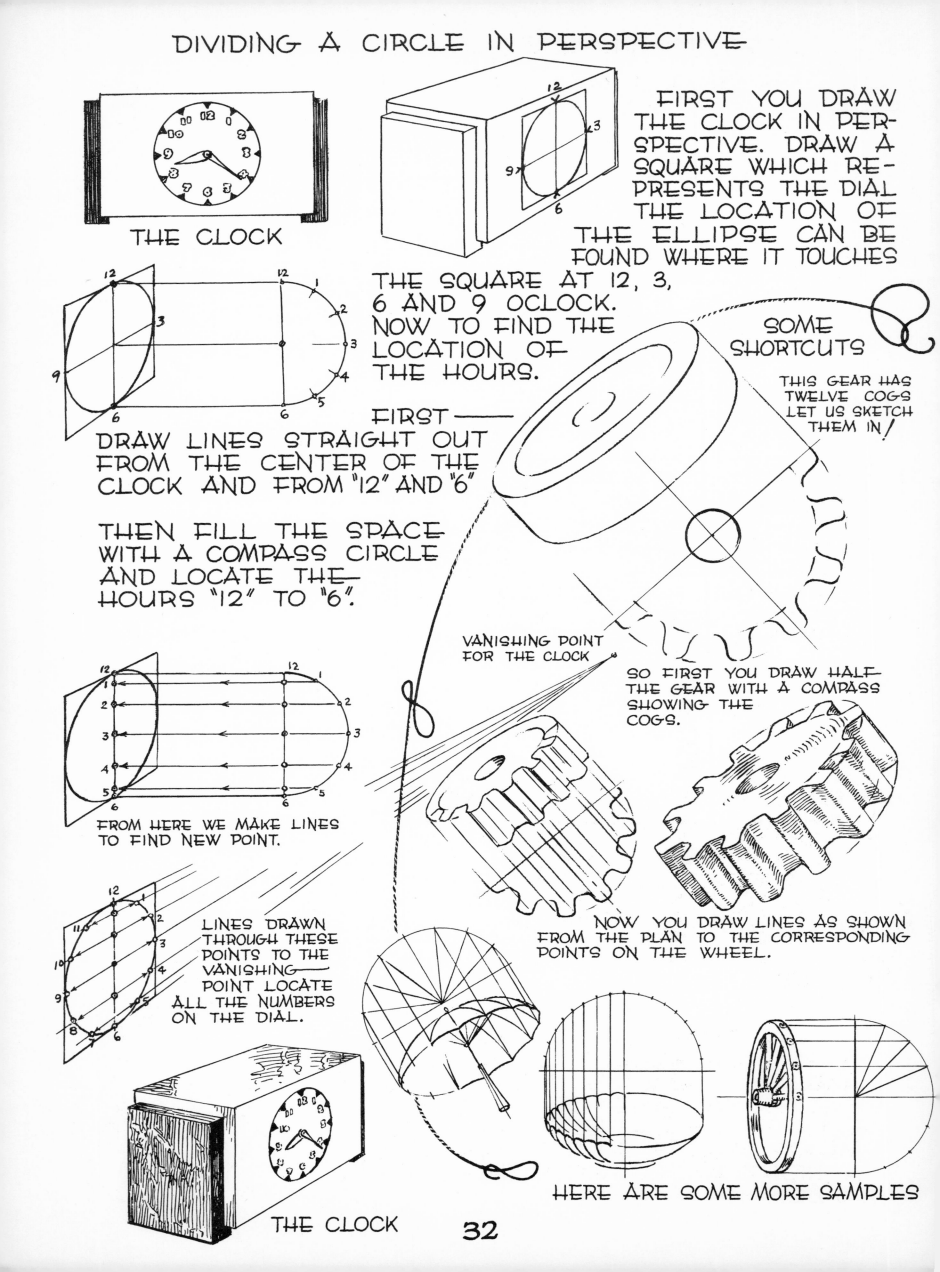

THE CLOCK

FIRST YOU DRAW THE CLOCK IN PERSPECTIVE. DRAW A SQUARE WHICH REPRESENTS THE DIAL THE LOCATION OF THE ELLIPSE CAN BE FOUND WHERE IT TOUCHES THE SQUARE AT 12, 3, 6 AND 9 OCLOCK. NOW TO FIND THE LOCATION OF THE HOURS.

FIRST—— DRAW LINES STRAIGHT OUT FROM THE CENTER OF THE CLOCK AND FROM "12" AND "6"

THEN FILL THE SPACE WITH A COMPASS CIRCLE AND LOCATE THE HOURS "12" TO "6".

SOME SHORTCUTS

THIS GEAR HAS TWELVE COGS LET US SKETCH THEM IN!

VANISHING POINT FOR THE CLOCK

SO FIRST YOU DRAW HALF THE GEAR WITH A COMPASS SHOWING THE COGS.

FROM HERE WE MAKE LINES TO FIND NEW POINT.

LINES DRAWN THROUGH THESE POINTS TO THE VANISHING POINT LOCATE ALL THE NUMBERS ON THE DIAL.

NOW YOU DRAW LINES AS SHOWN FROM THE PLAN TO THE CORRESPONDING POINTS ON THE WHEEL.

HERE ARE SOME MORE SAMPLES

THE CLOCK

PERSPECTIVE SPACING

EIGHT BOOKS

THE SIDE OF A BOX CAN BE DIVIDED INTO EQUAL HORIZONTAL PARTS.

DRAW A DIAGONAL AND NOTE WHERE IT CROSSES THE HORIZONTAL LINES. LINES DRAWN UPRIGHT THROUGH THESE POINTS WILL DIVIDE THE AREA INTO THE SAME NUMBER OF UPRIGHT PARTS.

THE SAME METHOD CAN BE USED WHEN THE SIDE OF THE BOX IS DRAWN IN PERSPECTIVE. THE UPRIGHT DIVISIONS ARE IN CORRECT LOCATION AND IN CORRECT PERSPECTIVE.

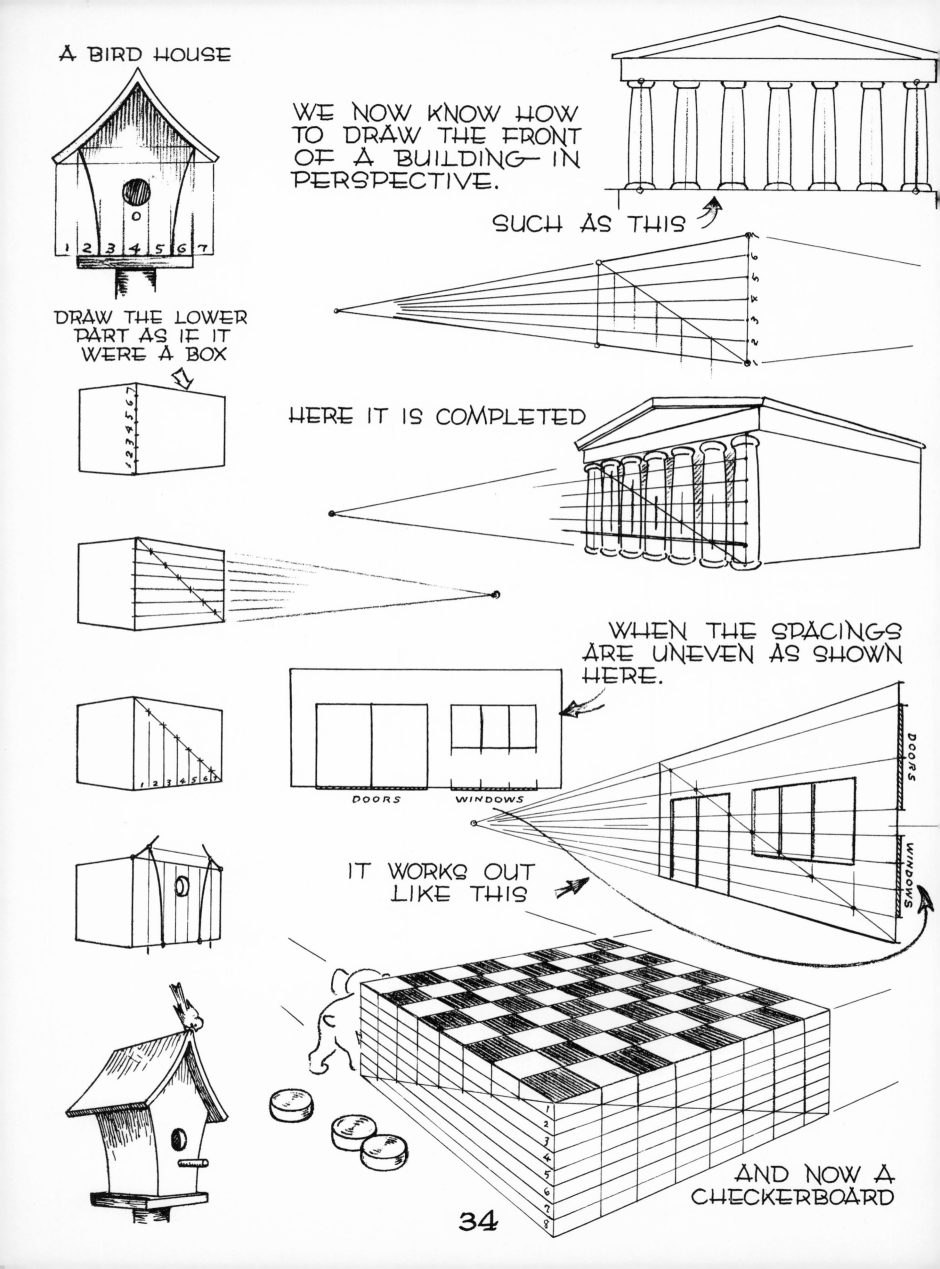

A BIRD HOUSE

1 2 3 4 5 6 7

DRAW THE LOWER PART AS IF IT WERE A BOX

1 2 3 4 5 6 7

WE NOW KNOW HOW TO DRAW THE FRONT OF A BUILDING IN PERSPECTIVE.

SUCH AS THIS

HERE IT IS COMPLETED

WHEN THE SPACINGS ARE UNEVEN AS SHOWN HERE.

DOORS   WINDOWS

IT WORKS OUT LIKE THIS

DOORS

WINDOWS

AND NOW A CHECKERBOARD

34

FIND THE CENTER

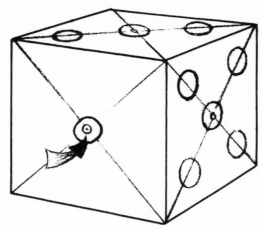

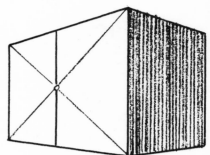

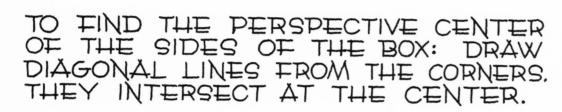

TO FIND THE PERSPECTIVE CENTER OF THE SIDES OF THE BOX: DRAW DIAGONAL LINES FROM THE CORNERS. THEY INTERSECT AT THE CENTER.

BOX DIVIDED INTO HALVES

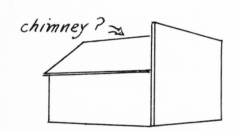

chimney ?

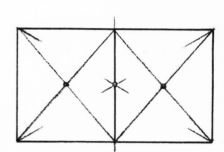

THE DOOR IS IN THE CENTER OF THE BUILDING FRONT. THE CHIMNEY IS IN THE CENTER OF THE ROOF.

INTO QUARTERS

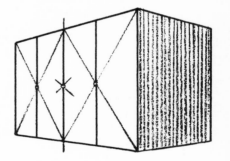

HERE ARE MORE CENTERS.

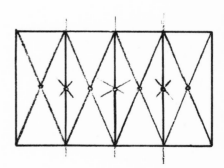

INTO EIGHTHS

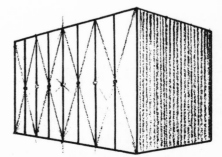

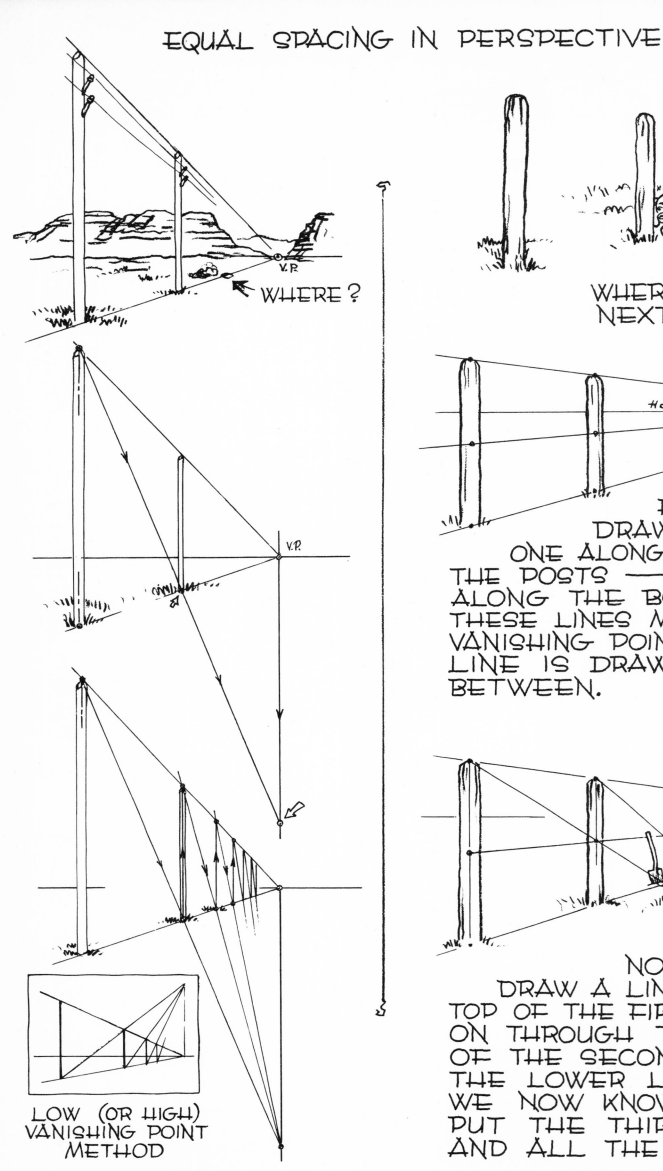

WHERE ?

V.P.

V.P.

LOW (OR HIGH)
VANISHING POINT
METHOD

WHERE DOES THE
NEXT POST GO ?

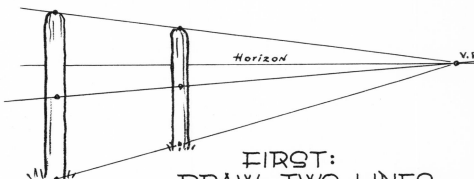

Horizon

V.P.

FIRST:
DRAW TWO LINES,
ONE ALONG THE TOP OF
THE POSTS — THE OTHER
ALONG THE BOTTOM.
THESE LINES MEET AT THE
VANISHING POINT. ANOTHER
LINE IS DRAWN HALFWAY
BETWEEN.

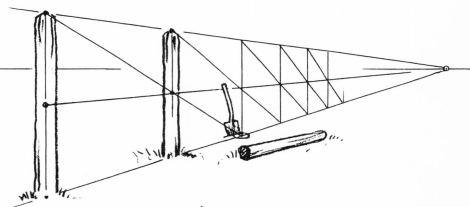

NOW:
DRAW A LINE FROM THE
TOP OF THE FIRST POST AND
ON THROUGH THE CENTER
OF THE SECOND POST TO
THE LOWER LINE.
WE NOW KNOW WHERE TO
PUT THE THIRD POST ——
AND ALL THE REST.

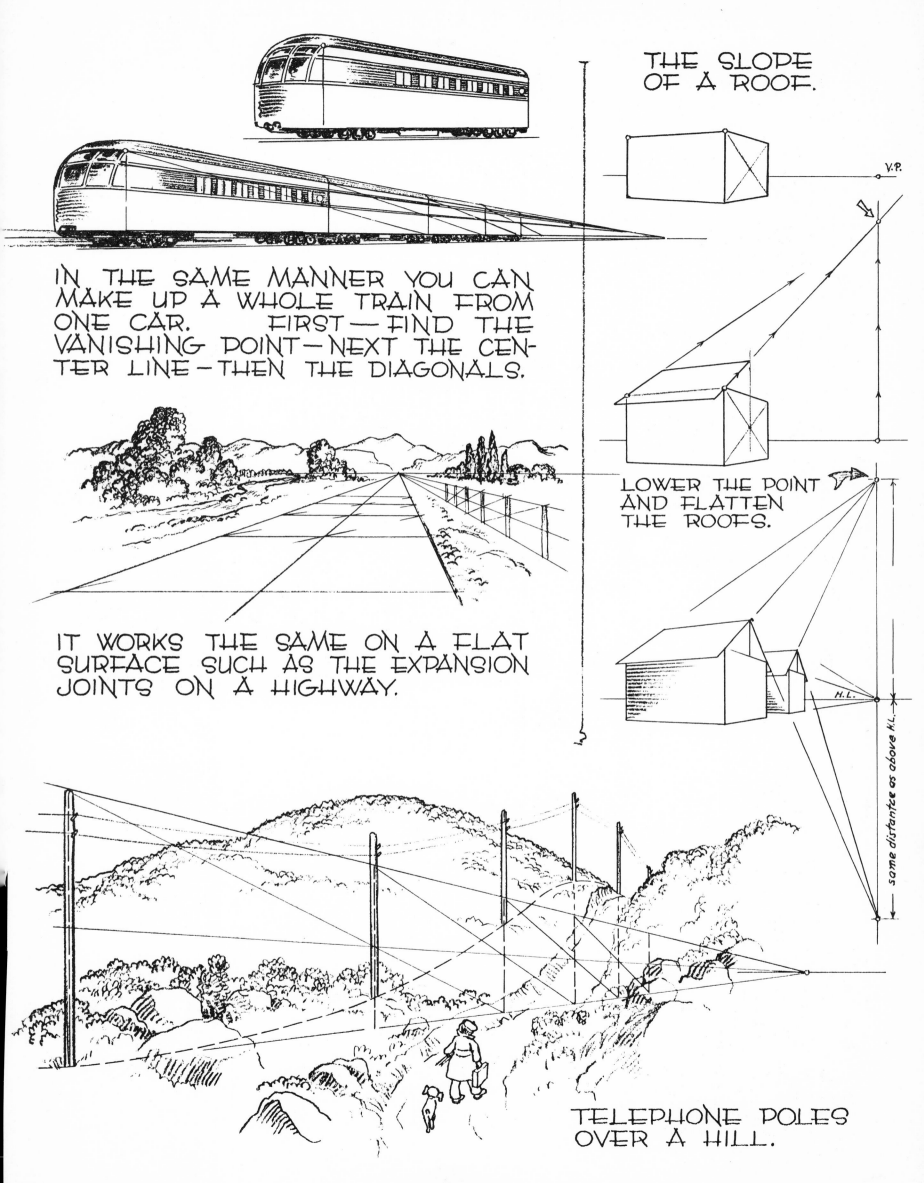

THE SLOPE OF A ROOF.

V.P.

IN THE SAME MANNER YOU CAN MAKE UP A WHOLE TRAIN FROM ONE CAR. FIRST — FIND THE VANISHING POINT — NEXT THE CENTER LINE — THEN THE DIAGONALS.

LOWER THE POINT AND FLATTEN THE ROOFS.

H.L.

same distance as above H.L.

IT WORKS THE SAME ON A FLAT SURFACE SUCH AS THE EXPANSION JOINTS ON A HIGHWAY.

TELEPHONE POLES OVER A HILL.

HEIGHTS OF PEOPLE NEAR AND FAR

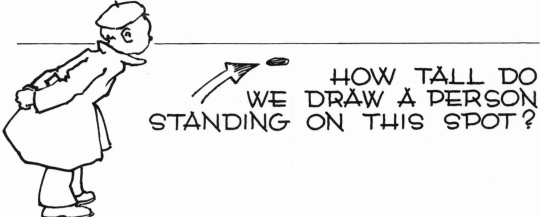

HOW TALL DO WE DRAW A PERSON STANDING ON THIS SPOT?

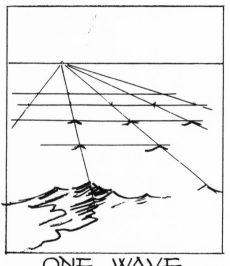

ONE SAGE BRUSH

FIRST — A LINE THROUGH THE SPOT TO THE HORIZON. WE START THE LINE AT THE MAN'S FEET.

MORE SAGE BRUSHES

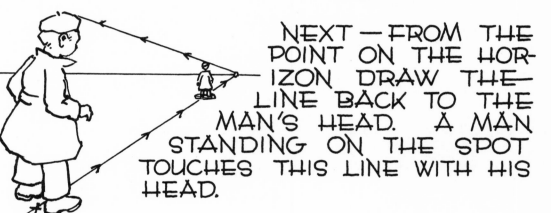

NEXT — FROM THE POINT ON THE HORIZON DRAW THE LINE BACK TO THE MAN'S HEAD. A MAN STANDING ON THE SPOT TOUCHES THIS LINE WITH HIS HEAD.

ONE WAVE

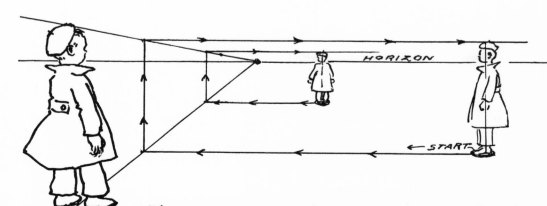

ANOTHER WAY IS BY DRAWING TWO LINES TO ANY POINT ON THE HORIZON. THEN START FROM THE SPOT AND DRAW THE HORIZONTAL AND PERPENDICULAR LINES SHOWN BY ARROW.

MORE WAVES

HEIGHTS OF PEOPLE

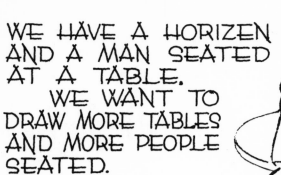

WE HAVE A HORIZEN AND A MAN SEATED AT A TABLE.
WE WANT TO DRAW MORE TABLES AND MORE PEOPLE SEATED.

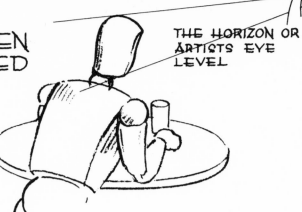

THE HORIZON OR ARTISTS EYE LEVEL

MEN MAY BE SHOWN HALF A HEAD TALLER THAN WOMEN

EYES ON HORIZON

LINES FROM THE MAN'S HEAD TO A POINT ON THE HORIZON GIVE THE HEIGHT OF
A HEAD AT ANY DISTANCE: "A" AND "B", FOR INSTANCE.

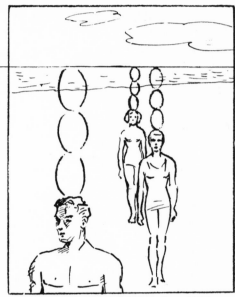

SAME NUMBER OF HEADS BELOW (OR ABOVE) THE HORIZON ~ ~ ~

ONE HEAD
ONE HALF HEAD
ONE HALF HEAD
ONE HEAD
1½ HEADS
1½ HEADS
1½ HEADS

ANOTHER METHOD
IF THE MEASUREMENT IS — SAY A HEAD AND A HALF BELOW THE HORIZON FOR ANY ONE HEAD—THEN ALL SEATED FIGURES CAN BE MEASURED IN THE SAME MANNER. STANDING FIGURES ARE MEASURED ABOVE THE HORIZON.

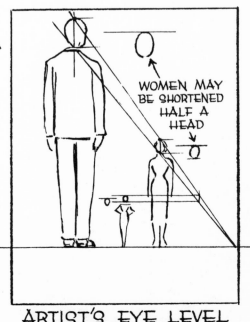

WOMEN MAY BE SHORTENED HALF A HEAD

ARTIST'S EYE LEVEL AT FLOOR LEVEL

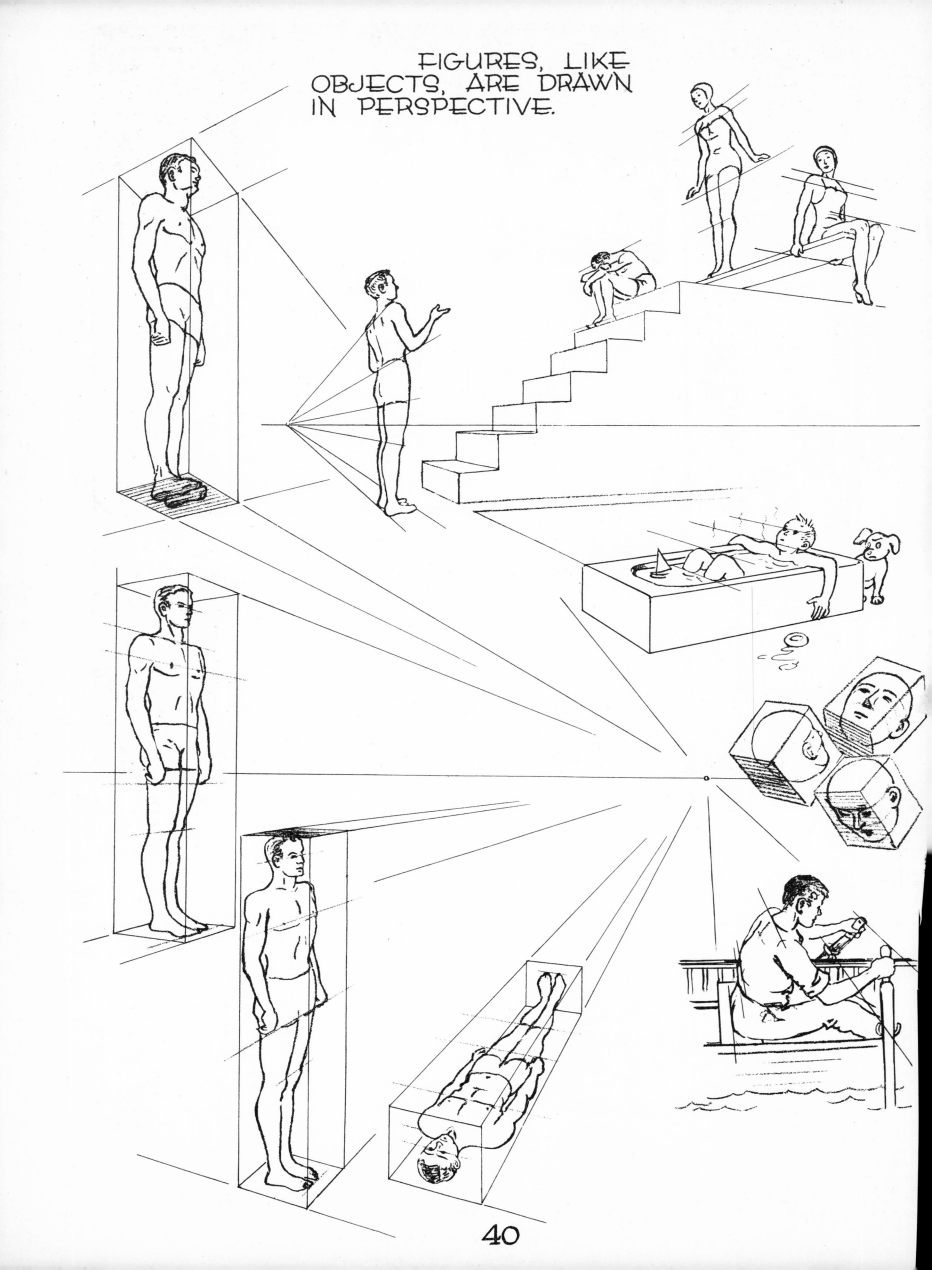

FIGURES, LIKE
OBJECTS, ARE DRAWN
IN PERSPECTIVE.